Leibniz on Purely Extrinsic Denominations

Rochester Studies in Philosophy
ISSN: 1529–188X
Senior Editor: Wade L. Robison
Rochester Institute of Technology

The Scottish Enlightenment: Essays in Reinterpretation
Edited by Paul Wood

Kant's Legacy: Essays in Honor of Lewis White Beck
Edited by Predrag Cicovacki

Plato's Erotic Thought: The Tree of the Unknown
Alfred Geier

Leibniz on Purely Extrinsic Denominations
Dennis Plaisted

LEIBNIZ ON PURELY EXTRINSIC DENOMINATIONS

Dennis Plaisted

University of Rochester Press

Copyright © 2002 Dennis Plaisted

All Rights Reserved. Except as permitted under current legislation, no part of this work may be photocopied, stored in a retrieval system, published, performed in public, adapted, broadcast, transmitted, recorded or reproduced in any form or by any means, without the prior permission of the copyright owner.

First published 2002

University of Rochester Press
668 Mt. Hope Avenue
Rochester, NY 14620   USA

and at Boydell & Brewer, Ltd
P.O. Box 9
Woodbridge, Suffolk IP12 3DF
United Kingdom
www.urpress.com

ISBN 1–58046–106–9

Library of Congress Cataloging-in-Publication Data

Plaisted, Dennis, 1965–
  Leibniz on purely extrinsic denominations / by Dennis Plaisted.
    p. cm. — (Rochester studies in philosophy ; 4)
  Includes bibliographical references and index.
  ISBN 1-58046-106-9 (alk. paper)
  1. Leibniz, Gottfried Wilhelm, Freiherr von, 1646–1716—
Contributionsin theory of relations.   2. Relation (Philosophy).
I. Title. II. Series.

B2599.R38 P53 2002
111-dc21
                                                                2002022510

British Library Cataloguing-in-Publication Data
A catalogue record for this book is
available from the British Library

Designed and typeset by Straight Creek Bookmakers
Printed in the United States of America
This publication is printed on acid-free paper

For my sweet love, Shabnam

Contents

Acknowledgments viii

Introduction 1

1 Two Views of Purely Extrinsic Denominations 3

2 Truth and Purely Extrinsic Denominations 13

3 Extrinsic Denominations and Where Accidents Are Allowed to Put Their Feet 35

4 Extrinsic Denominations and the Interconnection of All Things 47

5 Extrinsic Denominations and the Foundations of Relation 69

6 Extrinsic Denominations and the Claim that Every Monad Expresses the Universe 83

Appendix: A Critique of Massimo Mugnai's Version of NPE 99

References 107

Abbreviations 109

Notes 111

Index 127

Acknowledgments

For their helpful comments on earlier drafts of this book (or portions thereof), I would like to thank Bill Forgie, Matt Hanser, Jack Sanders, Tim Engström, Wade Robison, Berit Brogaard, and especially Tony Anderson and Patrick Riley. Additional thanks go to Wade Robison, the senior editor of the University of Rochester Press philosophy series, who first suggested that I attempt to publish this material in book form. Finally, I could not have completed this project without the constant love and support of my wife, Shabnam.

Introduction

Leibniz says that one of his most important doctrines and, indeed, one of the most important doctrines in all of philosophy, as well as theology, is his doctrine that there are no purely extrinsic denominations (hereafter referred to as NPE).[1] Unfortunately, despite his view of the importance of the doctrine, he nowhere offers an explicit statement as to what he meant by it. Nevertheless, on the basis of the way he employs the doctrine in various contexts and in the light of various other pronouncements by him which seem to be related to the doctrine, scholars have constructed interpretations of the claim. One such interpretation, which perhaps enjoys a modest consensus among interpreters, is that NPE is a claim that all extrinsic denominations reduce to intrinsic ones. For the moment, we may characterize extrinsic denominations as, roughly, relational properties and intrinsic denominations as non-relational properties. Thus, NPE, on the reductionist view, is that all relational properties reduce to non-relational ones. The sort of reduction these interpreters typically have in mind is that the truth of any extrinsic denomination that relates A to B can be inferred from the intrinsic denominations of A and B. The only sort of properties things actually have are intrinsic denominations; extrinsic denominations are not genuine properties of things, except in the derivative, reductionist sense just described. Critics of this interpretation have argued that the textual case for reductionism is inconclusive at best,[2] and I share this assessment with them. However, to my mind, a satisfactory *non-reductionist* account of what Leibniz meant by NPE has not been offered.[3] It is one thing to cast doubt on the reductionist understanding of NPE; it is quite another to explain, in a plausible non-reductionist way, what Leibniz *did* mean when he put forth the claim. My primary goal in this work is to provide such a non-reductionist account.

It is my contention that NPE, far from being a claim of the reducibility of extrinsic denominations, is actually an assertion that extrinsic denominations are genuine properties of the things they denominate. Specifically, NPE is the claim that there are no (true) extrinsic denominations of a thing that are not included in the concept of that thing. My interpretation of NPE thus essentially stands the reductionist reading on its head.

To establish my reading of NPE, I examine a line of textual evidence to which interpreters have inexplicably paid little attention: the way Leibniz argues for NPE and the way he argues from NPE to other conclusions. In some passages, he derives NPE from his predicate-in-subject principle of truth.[4] In other places, he employs his doctrine of the interconnection of all things to reach NPE.[5] He also bases his NPE claim on the principle of the identity of indiscernibles.[6] In addition, Leibniz employs NPE as *a premise* to establish his claim that each monad expresses every other. Though, as noted, he does not explicitly define NPE, Leibniz has much to say by way of explicit definition, or at least description, of each of these four principles, and so a consideration of what version of NPE displays the best inferential fit with these principles would likely prove illuminating. In the case of each argument, I attempt to show that my interpretation of NPE is the conclusion naturally suggested by the given principle, or, in the case of Leibniz's doctrine of expression, is the premise that most naturally leads to the given principle, while the reductionist version of NPE forms only an awkward, textually implausible fit with it.

The book is for the most part organized around the comparative reconstruction of the four arguments. I devote a chapter to each and these discussions comprise chapters two, four, five and six. In addition, chapter one sets forth in greater detail the reductionist interpretation of NPE, along with an analysis of the texts that are typically offered in support of it. I also set forth the alternative interpretation of NPE that I develop in the subsequent chapters. Chapter three responds to a recent objection advanced by Jan Cover and John Hawthorne which maintains that allowing extrinsic denominations to be genuine properties violates Leibniz's doctrine of individual accidents. Lastly, in the Appendix, I present a critique of the interpretation of NPE offered by Massimo Mugnai in his book, *Leibniz' Theory of Relations*. I believe that the four arguments I examine offer the most direct insight into how Leibniz understood NPE. The result of the examination is an original and serious critique of the reductionist reading of NPE (and Mugnai's), as well as the development of a far more plausible understanding of that claim. Finally, the book, by exploring the inferential connections between NPE and these other important Leibnizian doctrines, also displays the very central place that NPE occupies in Leibniz's metaphysics as a whole.[7]

Chapter One

Two Views of Purely Extrinsic Denominations

I. Introduction

This chapter introduces the two views of NPE that will be the focus of the book. I first describe in more detail the reductionist reading of NPE. Next, I examine the principal lines of textual evidence to which reductionists appeal to support their view. I conclude from this examination that the textual case for reductionism falls well short of being persuasive. Lastly, I set forth the view of NPE that I will defend throughout the book. I maintain that NPE is the assertion that there are no extrinsic denominations of a thing that are not included in the concept of that thing.

II. The Reductionist Reading

In order to get clear on the reductionist interpretation of NPE, we must first understand how reductionists, on Leibniz's behalf, define the term "extrinsic denomination" and its companion term "intrinsic denomination." Leibniz never favors us with an explicit definition of either term, but interpreters appear fairly confident that they can reconstruct Leibniz's understanding of these terms from the way he employs them in various contexts. Mates's reconstruction of these terms is perhaps the most precise:

> In the so-called region of ideas, the counterparts of definite or indefinite descriptions (or abbreviation of such) are *denominations*. Thus, the ontological status of denominations is that of concepts; in short, denomination is a kind of concept. Now, suppose that a given individual *I* falls under a given denomination *D*. If one of the descriptions with which *D* is correlated makes a reference, via a name or a quantified variable,[1] to some individual or individuals other than *I*, then *D* is called an 'extrinsic denomination' of *I*. Otherwise, *D* is called an 'intrinsic denomination' of *I*.[2]

So, for example, the denomination expressed by the definite description "the father of Solomon" would be an extrinsic denomination of David, as the description refers to an individual (viz., Solomon) other than David; whereas, the denomination expressed by the description "a man" would be an intrinsic denomination of David, since (apparently) the description makes no reference to other individuals.

With this terminology in hand, we can now consider what, according to those who espouse the reductionist interpretation, Leibniz thought a purely extrinsic denomination was. Reductionist interpreters claim that, for Leibniz, a purely extrinsic denomination is an extrinsic denomination that does not reduce to an intrinsic denomination,[3] and that when Leibniz says there are none of these, he means that all extrinsic denominations are reducible to intrinsic denominations. Now, it is extremely important to understand the sort of reduction that these interpreters have in mind. Consider the proposition,

(1) Andrew is taller than Bernard.

Under typical reductionist accounts, the extrinsic denomination <taller than Bernard>[4] (or perhaps more correctly <a person who is taller than Bernard>) would reduce to intrinsic denominations, some of which would be intrinsic denominations of Andrew and some of which would be intrinsic denominations of Bernard, and from which the truth of (1) could be *inferred*. Suppose Andrew has the intrinsic denomination <six feet tall> and Bernard has the intrinsic denomination <five and a half feet tall>. Since it is true that a) Andrew is six feet tall and b) Bernard is five and a half feet tall, one can infer, though perhaps not formally,[5] that (1) is true. Thus, <taller than Bernard>, though it truly denominates Andrew, is not a property of Andrew that is included in his complete individual concept.[6] Andrew's concept only contains intrinsic denominations, and a sufficiently discerning mind, examining Andrew's concept and also Bernard's, could simply infer that <taller than Bernard> is true of Andrew. The result of reducing (1) is thus not a set of propositions which together are logically equivalent to (1), but rather a set of propositions from which (1) follows.[7] This, according to Mates and others, is what Leibniz has in mind when he says there are no purely extrinsic denominations.

III. The Textual Case for Reductionism

In this section I canvass the main lines of textual evidence adduced by reductionists in support of their case. I identify five basic strands of texts that reductionists most commonly appeal to in support of their view, and I attempt to show with regard to each that it provides little or no support for the reductionist interpretation.[8]

One line of textual support for reductionism, generally credited to Bertrand Russell,[9] is that Leibniz's commitment to the reducibility of extrinsic denominations follows from his apparent commitment to the idea that every proposition either has a subject and a predicate, or is reducible to one that does. It is plausible to attribute this view of propositions to Leibniz. His doctrine of truth, for instance, would seem to suggest adherence to such a view. For Leibniz, a proposition is true just in case its predicate is contained in its subject,[10] and this would seem to suggest that if a proposition is to have truth value (and, ultimately, be meaningful), it must have a subject and a predicate that is or is not included in that subject. Assuming, at any rate, that Leibniz held such a view, it is supposed to entail a commitment to reductionism because, it is alleged, Leibniz did not regard extrinsic denominations as genuine predicates. Thus, any assertion involving an extrinsic denomination must reduce to a proposition or propositions that do have genuine predicates. And, of course, only intrinsic denominations can serve as genuine predicates here.

As I shall argue at length in chapter two, the central problem with the foregoing lies in the claim that Leibniz did not regard extrinsic denominations as genuine predicates. There is simply no textual evidence to support such a claim, and, in fact, there is a significant amount of evidence directly to the contrary. I set forth this evidence in chapter two and also respond to an objection to the interpretation I offer of it recently advanced by Jan Cover and John Hawthorne.

The second line of evidence involves passages where Leibniz appears to analyze and rewrite relational assertions in terms of non-relational ones. In one passage, for example, Leibniz analyzes the relational claim "Peter is similar to Paul" into the two claims "Peter is A now" and "Paul is A now,"[11] where A is presumably some intrinsic denomination that is true of both Peter and Paul.[12] Despite appearances, however, these passages provide little support for the reductionist reading of NPE. First of all, Leibniz never offers these analyses in the context of NPE; he typically offers them in his writings on grammatical analysis. Leibniz never suggests in these settings that he is attempting to reduce relational propositions to non-relational ones; rather, he says that these analyses should be carried out so that certain intuitively valid arguments can be handled by the accepted logical methods of his day. Leibniz and his contemporaries did not possess a logic of relations, and Leibniz was apparently rather conservative in his attitude toward developing new techniques for logic. Consider the following:

> All oblique inferences—e.g. 'Peter is similar to Paul, therefore Paul is similar to Peter'—are to be explained by explanations of words; it is reduced to the propositions 'Peter is A now' and 'Paul is A now'.[13]

The relation of similarity is symmetric, and so if Peter is similar to Paul, we should be able to infer that Paul is similar to Peter. But Leibniz had no way of rendering the symmetry of a relation as an explicit premise in an argument. Now, the quote does not make clear how the proposed analysis of similarity allows the inference to go through under the accepted logic of Leibniz's day,[14] but it does show that the analysis had a purpose other than what reductionists would claim for it. Elsewhere, immediately after offering similar analyses of relational propositions, Leibniz states that unless we perform these translations, we "will never escape without being compelled . . . to invent new ways of reasoning."[15] Since such was Leibniz's stated purpose for the translations, the fact that he offers these translations is at best inconclusive evidence for the reductionist reading of NPE.

A second reason for rejecting these passages as evidence for reductionism is that in many instances Leibniz's analyses of relational claims do not terminate in non-relational ones. Consider his analysis of "Paris is the lover of Helen," which is, "'Paris loves, and by that very fact Helen is loved' . . . .or, 'Paris is a lover, and by that very fact Helen is a loved one.'"[16] The denominations <a lover> and <a loved one> are both transparently extrinsic: they imply the existence of another individual to which the denominated individual is related. Thus, if Leibniz was attempting in these translations to show the reducibility of extrinsic denominations to intrinsic ones, his attempt was an unmitigated failure. It makes far more sense to think that Leibniz was not seeking a reduction of relational to non-relational propositions, but instead to think, as explained in the preceding paragraph, that he was attempting to fit intuitively valid arguments into existing modes of reasoning. These translations, then, provide little or no support for the reductionist reading of NPE.

Another strand of the reductionist textual case draws upon Leibniz's oft-repeated assertion that relations are mere mental entities. Leibniz is well known to have regarded only two sorts of things as real: substances and their accidents. As a result, he says that a relation, "being neither a substance nor an accident . . . must be a mere ideal thing, the consideration of which is nevertheless useful."[17] Leibniz does not make clear why relations cannot be substances (he probably found such an idea unthinkable), but he does explain why relations cannot be accidents. Leibniz held that accidents are *individual* to the substance that has them, which is to say that a given accident cannot be in more than one substance.[18] Yet relations always involve more than one substance, and so if a relation were permitted as an accident "we should have an accident in two subjects, with one leg in one and the other leg in the other, which is contrary to the notion of accidents."[19] Kulstad explains the use this doctrine is put to by reductionists in this way:

> Leibniz believes that relations are mere ideal things; he must, therefore, believe that relational propositions, which suggest that relations are genuine constituents of the world, are misleading with respect to what actually exists; it is natu-

ral to assume that he would want to reduce such propositions to ones which are not misleading with respect to what exists; . . . it seems likely that he would employ subject-predicate propositions in such a reduction [where "predicate" is understood as a non-relational predicate].[20]

But, as Kulstad and others have pointed out,[21] the problem with putting forward this line of Leibniz's thinking in support of the reducibility of extrinsic denominations is that it ignores a distinction which Leibniz undeniably, though not in so many words, draws between relations *simpliciter* and relational accidents. All of Leibniz's pronouncements concerning the ideality of relations and their inability to serve as attributes are directed at relations *simpliciter*, not relational accidents. In fact, Leibniz appears to assert plainly that relational accidents can be genuine accidents of things. The following quote from Leibniz's *Correspondence with Clarke* demonstrates these points very well:

> The ratio or proportion between two lines L and M may be conceived in three ways: as a ratio of the greater L to the lesser M, as a ratio of the lesser M to the greater L, and, lastly, as something abstracted from both, that is, the ratio between L and M without considering which is the antecedent or which the consequent, which the subject and which the object. . . . In the first way of considering, L the greater, in the second, M the lesser, is the subject of that accident which philosophers call "relation." But which of them will be the subject in the third way of considering them? It cannot be said that both of them, L and M together, are the subject of such an accident; for, if so, we should have an accident in two subjects, one with one leg in one and the other in the other . . . . Therefore we must say that this relation, in this third way of considering it, is indeed out of the subjects; but being neither a substance nor an accident, it must be a mere mental thing, the consideration of which is nevertheless useful.[22]

For ease of discussion, let us suppose that line L is twice as long as line M. Leibniz says we can regard this situation in three different ways:

(2) L is twice as long as M (the ratio of L to M).
(3) M is half as long as L (the ratio of M to L).
(4) The ratio between M's length and L's is 2:1

Then Leibniz says that when we look at the matter from the standpoint of (2) and (3), we see that L and M are both subjects "of that accident which philosophers call 'relation'." This statement appears to be nothing less than a straightforward statement that certain relations can be accidents. And, given the way Leibniz describes cases (2) and (3), I believe we can say that this means L has the accident "twice as long as M" and M has the accident "half as long as L." Of course, the concepts of those two accidents are extrinsic denominations that (if these two accidents are truly respective accidents of L and M) will be in the respective concepts of L and M. But the situation in (4) is that of a relation *simpliciter*, the bare numeric ratio between L's length and M's length. This relation runs afoul of Leibniz's doctrine of individual accidents and thus is purely ideal. Unfortunately, Leibniz affixes the term "relation" to all three cases. Nevertheless, it is clear from the passage that he does regard what we have been calling relational accidents differently from relations *simpliciter*, saying that the former are genuine accidents, while the latter are not.

Jan Cover and John Hawthorne have recently argued, however, that if we allow relational accidents as *bona fide* accidents, and their corresponding extrinsic denominations as properties, then a similar and quite serious problem will still lie against us. Consider once again the extrinsic denomination <father of Solomon>. Since this is a true extrinsic denomination of David, and if extrinsic denominations are included in the concepts of what they denominate, then that denomination is included in David's concept. Now, according to Leibniz, concept-inclusion is a transitive relation.[23] And it would seem that <Solomon> is included in <father of Solomon>. So, if <father of Solomon> is included in <David>, then it would seem that <Solomon> is included in <David>. In effect, it is claimed that <Solomon> becomes a property in David's concept, and Solomon (the substance) becomes a constituent of an accident of David. As Cover and Hawthorne put the point, "are we to believe that he [Leibniz] rejects accidents with one leg in one substance and the other in another, but welcomes accidents with one leg in one substance and a full-nelson hug around another?"[24] The problem is further aggravated by the fact that Leibniz held to what might be termed an Aristotelian view of substance. Leibniz says, "when several predicates are attributed to one and the same subject, and this subject is not attributed to any other, one calls this subject an individual substance."[25] Leibniz, then, would almost certainly not allow the predication of Solomon to David that seems to result here. If such were the consequence of recognizing extrinsic denominations as properties, then the claim that Leibniz recognized them as such would be highly questionable. I am convinced, though, that this objection utterly fails, for although concept-inclusion is transitive, the antecedent conditions of transitivity are not met in this or, indeed, any other example like it. Though <father of Solomon> is included in David's concept, <Solomon> is not included in <father of Solomon>, and thus we cannot, via the transitivity of inclusion, infer that <Solomon> is a property of David. An adequate showing of this somewhat surprising result requires consideration of Leibniz's views on the formal properties of concept-inclusion and the structure of complex concepts. Such a showing exceeds the scope of the present chapter, but is presented at length in chapter three.

A fourth and more indirect line of reductionist evidence invokes Leibniz's claim that the states of one substance do not depend on the states of any other, or as Leibniz phrases it, each substance is "a world apart . . . as if there existed nothing but God and itself."[26] The point of this objection is not easy to determine but it seems to be something like the following. If Leibniz were to allow relational accidents in substances, then the states of a substance would depend on other substances, since the applicability of such an accident would depend on other substances existing and having the states that are relevant to the relation. But since Leibniz clearly states that the states of a substance do not depend on the states of others, Leibniz did not allow relational accidents.[27] This objection, however, rests on a misapprehension of the world-apart doctrine. Leibniz's descriptions of that doctrine do not set up a blanket prohibition on any type of substantial dependence whatever. The only sort of dependence they expressly disallow is *causal* dependence. Each monad's states arise by means of its own "internal law" and not by the causal influence of other monads.[28] That a thing has relational attributes in no way implies that other monads causally influence it. As long as its relational attributes, along with all its other attributes, arise through the unfolding of its own internal law and not the causal impact of other monads, then the allowance of relational attributes does not violate the world apart doctrine. The mistake in this reductionist line of reasoning is nicely summarized by Fred D'Agostino:

> This argument is attractive but is, I think, fallacious. The fallacy lies in mistaking logical for causal dependence. The value of a relational predicate is of course logically dependent on all of its arguments. But this is not to say that the substance described by that predicate is causally dependent on other substances. If all substances exist in a pre-established harmony, . . . then predicates characteristic of one substance could be logically dependent on—in the sense of reflecting changes in—other substances, without this implying any causal interaction between these substances.[29]

Leibniz's denial of causal interaction between monads thus provides no grounds for thinking he did not permit relational accidents to inhere in things.

The fifth and, in my opinion, most plausible piece of textual evidence in the reductionist arsenal is Leibniz's frequent statement that extrinsic denominations are founded on intrinsic denominations. Some of the passages most often cited by reductionists in this regard are these:

> To be in a place is not a bare extrinsic denomination; indeed, there is no denomination so extrinsic that it does not have an intrinsic denomination as its basis.[30]

> In general, place, position and quantity, such as number and proportion, are merely relations, and result from other things which by themselves either con-

stitute or terminate a change . . . .[T]hey are mere results, which do not constitute any intrinsic denomination per se, and so they are merely relations which demand a foundation from the category of quality, that is, from an intrinsic accidental denomination.[31]

On their surfaces, these passages admittedly display a distinctly reductionist flavor. The reductionist construal of NPE maintains that extrinsic denominations are not properties of the things they denominate. Things only have intrinsic denominations as properties. That a given extrinsic denomination holds of an individual can be inferred from the intrinsic denominations of that individual and the intrinsic denominations of the individual to which the extrinsic denomination relates the denominated individual. This understanding of the relationship between extrinsic and intrinsic denominations seemingly provides a fairly natural way to construe Leibniz's claim that extrinsic denominations are founded on intrinsic ones.

These texts do not provide the strong support for reductionism that they initially seem to, however. Invoking the earlier distinction between relations simpliciter and relational properties seriously undermines their reductionistic evidential value. Leibniz, as seen earlier, affixes the term "relation" to both relations simpliciter and relational properties, while at the same time drawing a clear distinction between the two, saying one can be a legitimate accident while the other cannot. He appears also to employ "extrinsic denomination" in the same manner, in some cases using it to refer to relations simpliciter and other times to refer to relational properties. When he says that extrinsic denominations are founded on intrinsic ones, the context nearly always makes clear that he is speaking of relations *simpliciter* being founded on intrinsic denominations not relational properties. A far more comprehensive showing of this comprises a good portion of chapter five, but for now consider the following passage:

I do not believe that you will admit an accident that is in two subjects at the same time. My judgment about relations is that paternity in David is one thing, sonship in Solomon another, but that the relation common to both is a merely mental thing *whose foundation is the modifications of the individuals*.[32]

This passage displays a structure strikingly similar to the one quoted above concerning the lengths of L and M that provided the grounds for distinguishing relations simpliciter from relational properties. <Paternity> and <sonship> are both plausibly reckoned as relational properties, and the passage suggests that they are "in" David and Solomon, respectively. But the relation common to both[33] is a mere mental thing, and it is *this* relation that is founded on the properties of the related individuals, not the extrinsic denominations of <paternity> and <sonship>. Hence, Leibniz's recurring claim that relations/extrinsic denominations are founded on intrinsic denominations does not offer the weighty support for reductionism that it appeared to initially. Indeed, as I will argue in chapter five, I believe that, for Leibniz, <paternity> and <sonship> are the very properties of the related individuals that provide the foundation for the common relation in this case. Now, since Leibniz says that relations are founded on intrinsic denominations, it will be incumbent upon me to explain how denominations such as <paternity> and <sonship> can be sensibly regarded as intrinsic denominations for these purposes. I argue that if my reading of NPE is correct, they are intrinsic denominations in the sense that they are in or are intrinsic to what they denominate. (See chapter five, sections II-IV, for the full demonstration of this point.)

The foregoing represents the bulk of the textual case for the reductionist position. None of the strands are individually compelling, and even considered together, they do not make a terribly potent showing. Each piece of evidence, I maintain, can be better explained in a non-reductionist manner. The door is open, then, for another understanding of NPE.[34]

IV. NPE as an Assertion that Extrinsic Denominations are Properties of What They Denominate

According to reductionists, the NPE claim is, at bottom, a claim that extrinsic denominations are not properties of things, as they reduce to intrinsic ones in the sense earlier described. I, however, understand the NPE claim in quite another manner. I believe NPE, in the end, actually amounts to the assertion that extrinsic denominations *are* genuine properties of things. According to the interpretation I am advancing, a purely extrinsic denomination is defined as follows:

(5) A purely extrinsic denomination of an individual is an extrinsic denomination (which truly denominates that individual) that is not included in that individual's concept.

And Leibniz's claim that there are no such denominations (i.e., NPE) becomes the claim that

(6) There are no extrinsic denominations of an individual (which truly denominate that individual) that are not included in that individual's concept.[35]

Now, how does (6), if true, show that extrinsic denominations are properties of things? Leibniz distinguishes between the concepts of an individual and the individual. The concepts of individuals are what Leibniz refers to as complete individual concepts.[36] The concepts that are included in an individual's concept are the properties of that individual.[37] Consequently, if an extrinsic denomination is included in the concept of the individual it denominates, it can be said to be a property of that individual.

Why should NPE be read in this way? As a modest beginning, I would point to a trend in Leibniz's usage of the term "extrinsic denomination" which suggests that he referred to extrinsic denominations as such because they were extrinsic to, or out of, what they denominate. In the *New Essays*, Leibniz writes:

> Suppose for instance that the imaginary 'Australians' swarmed into our latitudes: it is likely that some way would be found of distinguishing them from us; but if not . . . then we should have to try to introduce artificial marks to distinguish the races from one another. No doubt there would be an *inner* difference, but since we should be unable to detect it we should have to rely solely on the extrinsic denomination of birth, and try to associate with it an indelible artificial mark which would provide an intrinsic denomination and a permanent means of telling our race apart from theirs.[38]

Leibniz here contrasts extrinsic denominations with what is in a thing. One natural way, therefore, of taking the claim that there are no purely extrinsic denominations is as a claim that there are no denominations of a thing that are simply out of that thing, and this is how (6) renders NPE. Of course, reductionists will gladly regard extrinsic denominations as out of what they denominate, but they will likely draw another implication from that fact concerning the meaning of NPE. According to them, the claim that there are no purely extrinsic denominations means that, though extrinsic denominations are out of what they denominate, they have a kind of foothold in what they denominate, as they reduce, at least in part, to denominations which are in the denominated thing. Thus, I do not claim that Leibniz's usage of "extrinsic denomination" to denote denominations that are extrinsic to what they denominate decidedly favors (6) as a reading of NPE over the reductionist view. Rather my claim, for the moment, is that his usage suggests (6) as at least one natural candidate for the meaning of NPE. The goal of the following chapters will be to establish the further result that (6) offers the most plausible rendering of NPE.

The thrust of these chapters is to demonstrate that (6) is the reading of NPE that can best serve as the conclusion of Leibniz's arguments for NPE. The conclusion most naturally suggested by Leibniz's arguments for NPE is that extrinsic denominations must be properties that are included in the concepts of what they denominate. This is also the understanding of NPE that would function best as a premise for the doctrine of expression. This is quite simply the result that Leibniz appears to have been seeking, or working with, in the context of these arguments. I will attempt to show, for each argument Leibniz gives, why this is so, and also why the reductionist reading of NPE is so unlikely to have been what Leibniz had in mind.

Chapter Two

Truth and Purely Extrinsic Denominations

I. Introduction

One of Leibniz's most important doctrines—perhaps *the* most important—is his predicate-in-subject theory of truth (hereafter referred to as PS). His PS principle can be stated as follows:

(7) A proposition is true if and only if its predicate concept is included in its subject concept.[1]

One concept's inclusion in another is a technical notion in Leibniz's philosophy. I shall have much more to say about Leibniz's notion of concept-inclusion in chapter three, but for now I will merely note that with regard to a predicate concept's inclusion in a subject concept, Leibniz says that

> The subject-term, therefore, must always include the predicate-term, in such a way that a man who understood the notion of the subject perfectly would also judge that the predicate belongs to it.[2]

So, if a predicate is included in a subject, then the predicate will be part of the very idea of the subject; it will not be possible to conceive of the subject completely without also conceiving the predicate. There are many fascinating issues surrounding Leibniz's PS doctrine of truth, such as whether, despite his pronouncements to the contrary, all true propositions become necessary truths if PS is accepted. However, the concern at present is how best to render his argument that because of PS, there are no purely extrinsic denominations. I will first offer a reconstruction of the argument with its conclusion interpreted as (6), and then I will offer a reconstruction of the argument with its conclusion read reductionistically. I maintain that reflection on the PS principle applied to propositions whose predicate concepts are extrinsic denominations straightforwardly implies that extrinsic denominations are *in* the subjects of which they are predicated, which is essentially what (6) maintains. I then argue that the reductionist version of NPE can provide at best an awkward and textually implausible reconstruction of the PS argument. Central to the reductionist reconstruction is a claim that the PS principle does not apply to propositions having extrinsic denominations as predicates. Some reductionists accept this claim on the ground that Leibniz did not regard extrinsic denominations as genuine predicates. Others seem to believe that Leibniz did regard extrinsic denominations as predicates, just not the sort of predicates to which PS can apply. I argue that neither contention has any textual merit, and so any reconstruction of the PS argument for NPE that relies on them is equally lacking in merit. In fact, the texts reductionists are likely to offer in support of these contentions are, I maintain, best understood as supporting the reading of NPE that I propose. Finally, once Leibniz derives NPE from PS, he goes on to infer the further result that whenever a thing's extrinsic denominations change, there is a change in that thing. I argue that this inference is highly plausible if NPE is interpreted as (6), but that it simply does not follow if NPE is read in a reductionist manner.

II. The PS Argument for NPE Interpreted as (6)

The clearest statement of the PS argument is found in Leibniz's essay *Primary Truths*:

> It also follows that there are no purely extrinsic denominations, which have no foundation in the thing denominated. For the notion of the subject denominated must involve the notion of the predicate; consequently, as often as the denomination of the thing is changed, there must be some variation in the thing itself.[3]

The argument is rather simple; its only explicit premise is the PS principle. And then from the conclusion that there are no purely extrinsic denominations, Leibniz goes on to derive the further result that "as often as the denomination of the thing is changed, there must be some variation in the thing itself."[4] As will be seen later, that Leibniz uses NPE to obtain this second consequence also sheds a good deal of light on how NPE should be understood. For now, I will confine my attention to the argument that because of the PS principle, there are no purely extrinsic denominations. I will first offer a reconstruction of the argument with its conclusion interpreted as (6) above, and then I will attempt to reconstruct the argument with its conclusion interpreted along reductionist lines. Comparison of the two will reveal that the reductionist reconstruction provides only a strained interpretation of the argument, one which relies upon textually implausible assumed premises, while the reconstruction leading to (6) requires no assumed premises and comports very well with the text.

From the way Leibniz presents the PS argument, one gets the impression that he regarded the NPE claim as a fairly immediate consequence of the PS principle. As I hope will become clear, if NPE is interpreted as (6) above, then NPE does indeed follow rather closely on the heels of the PS principle. To see why this is so, consider the following passage, given—not insignificantly—just two paragraphs prior to the above quote of the PS argument, in which Leibniz states the PS principle and comments on the types of propositions to which it applies:

> The predicate or consequent, therefore, is always in the subject or antecedent, and this constitutes the nature of truth in general, or, the connexion between the terms of a proposition . . . .But this is true in the case of every affirmative truth, universal or particular, necessary or contingent, *and in the case of both an intrinsic and an extrinsic denomination* [emphasis added].[5]

Though it is correct to speak of universal propositions or necessary propositions, intrinsic and extrinsic denominations are not *types* of propositions; they are properties. So, it seems clear that Leibniz is here speaking of propositions *involving* intrinsic or extrinsic denominations. And by this I believe that Leibniz means that the PS principle is the basis of truth for propositions whose *predicates* (or, more correctly, predicate concepts) are intrinsic or extrinsic denominations.

With this observation in hand, we can now formulate the argument from PS to NPE, with NPE interpreted as (6). If PS is the basis of truth for propositions whose predicate concepts are extrinsic denominations, then it would seem to follow rather immediately that

(8) If a true proposition has an extrinsic denomination as its predicate concept, then that extrinsic denomination is included in the concept of the subject (that is, in the concept of the thing denominated).

And, given (8), we can say that there are no extrinsic denominations of a thing which are not included in the concept of that thing, and this, of course, is exactly what (6) maintains. An extrinsic denomination truly denominates an individual just in case the proposition whose subject concept is the concept of that individual and whose predicate concept is that extrinsic denomination is true. And, according to PS, that proposition is true just in case that extrinsic denomination is included in the concept of that individual. An extrinsic denomination truly denominates an individual, therefore, just in case that denomination is included in the concept of that individual. Hence, (6). Thus, once Leibniz, in his *Primary Truths*, informs us that PS is the basis of the truth of all propositions including those whose predicate concepts are extrinsic denominations, he can then simply say, as indeed he does in that essay, that "there are no purely extrinsic denominations . . . [f]or the notion of the subject denominated must involve the notion of the predicate." He can, that is, if the NPE claim is understood as (6).

I noted earlier that once Leibniz establishes NPE from PS (in the above passage from *Primary Truths*), he then appears to infer the further conclusion that

(9) As often as the denomination of the thing is changed, there must be some variation in the thing itself.

I will now show how natural the move to this second consequence is when NPE is interpreted as (6). As earlier discussed, the upshot of NPE when read as (6) is that extrinsic denominations are really in, or are genuine properties of, the things they denominate. And thus it follows immediately that anytime the denomination of a thing is changed, there will be a change among the properties that are included in the concept of the thing as well, which, for Leibniz, undoubtedly signals a change in the thing itself. So, not only is (6) a straightforward consequence of PS, but it can also serve as a premise from which (9) can be immediately inferred. As will soon become evident, the reductionist version of NPE does not fare nearly as well.

III. A Reductionist Version of the PS Argument

I would now like to suggest a reductionist version of the PS argument. I know of no actual attempt by a reductionist to reconstruct this argument, and so I cannot be entirely sure that the version I offer is one that reductionists would endorse. However, I will present considerations which, I believe, show that the version I offer is likely along the general lines of a reconstruction that a reductionist would offer. Comparison of the proposed reductionist version with the non-reductionist one offered above will reveal that the reductionist version is far less plausible as an interpretation of Leibniz than its non-reductionist counterpart.

The preceding reconstruction of the PS argument explicitly relies on the claim that the PS principle of truth is applicable to propositions whose predicate concepts are extrinsic denominations; and, of course, once this claim was asserted, it was a small step to infer (6). I believe it is unlikely, however, that a reductionist would concede the applicability of PS to propositions having extrinsic denominations as predicate concepts. The reason for this is that certain well-known interpreters of Leibniz have claimed that he did not regard extrinsic denominations as genuine predicates or did not regard propositions containing them as being in so-called subject-predicate form (where a proposition is in subject-predicate form just in case it has a subject concept and a predicate concept).[6] And this would mean that Leibniz would not have viewed the PS criterion of truth as being applicable to such propositions, as

PS, it would seem, could only meaningfully apply to propositions that have a subject and a predicate. Thus, the move to (8) in my earlier reconstruction of the PS argument would likely be explicitly rejected by reductionists.

Whether or not it is plausible to attribute to Leibniz the belief that PS is inapplicable to propositions containing extrinsic denominations is a question I will come to shortly. For now, I simply want to note the reductionists' probable denial of the PS criterion's applicability to propositions containing extrinsic denominations, as I believe that this denial will be central to a reductionist rendering of the PS argument for NPE. Indeed, I cannot see how the reductionist can proceed here if PS is applicable to such propositions. If extrinsic denominations can serve as predicate concepts in propositions and such propositions are true because their predicate concepts are included in their subject concepts, then how is it that PS drives us to the conclusion that extrinsic denominations reduce to intrinsic ones? If PS is applicable to such propositions, then as was shown above, that would seem to imply that extrinsic denominations are included in the complete concepts of individuals, which is plainly inconsistent with the pronouncements of many reductionists that complete individual concepts include only intrinsic denominations.[7] For example, if PS is applicable to "Alexander is the conqueror of Darius," then <the conqueror of Darius> would seem to be included in Alexander's concept, and that certainly would not be a welcome result to reductionists. I suppose someone may attempt to make the somewhat strange claim that though extrinsic denominations, by PS, are so included, they still, according to some other principle, reduce to intrinsic denominations, so that in the end the only denominations that appear in complete individual concepts are intrinsic ones. But it is difficult to see what such a principle would be. Furthermore, whatever principle is put forward is utterly indispensable to the argument. Why did Leibniz not say what it was? Perhaps there is some way of obtaining the reductionist result here, but I just cannot see what it would be. Thus, I believe that to provide a reasonable reconstruction of the PS argument that leads to their version of NPE, reductionists will have to deny the PS principle's direct applicability to propositions involving extrinsic denominations.

Yet if PS is not applicable to propositions involving extrinsic denominations and PS is Leibniz's *only* criterion for the truth of a proposition, then what of the truth-value of such propositions or even their very meaningfulness? Intuitively, at least, when I utter a statement such as "David is the father of Solomon," I seem to say something that is both meaningful and true and I believe a reductionist would share this intuition. However, given the apparent inapplicability of PS to such a proposition, the intuition begins to seem questionable. There is an apparent tension, then, in holding that (a) PS is the sole criterion of truth, (b) PS has no application to propositions involving extrinsic denominations, and (c) propositions involving extrinsic denominations can be true or false. I believe that the reductionist will put forward the claim that extrinsic denominations reduce to intrinsic denominations as the only way out of this seeming conflict. Propositions whose predicate concepts are *intrinsic* denominations *can* be true as a result of their predicate concepts being included in their subject concepts. Thus, if the truth of propositions involving extrinsic denominations can be inferred from a set of propositions all of whose members have intrinsic denominations for predicate concepts, then we will be able to recognize propositions involving extrinsic denominations as true while still denying the direct applicability of PS to those propositions. As discussed earlier, once we give up, as many reductionists do, the idea that extrinsic denominations can serve as genuine predicate concepts, we render PS incapable of (directly, at least) serving as the standard of truth for propositions containing extrinsic denominations. What results from this, in turn, is the tension described above in statements (a)–(c), and the reductionist version of the NPE claim is advanced as the resolution of this tension. This, I feel is along the general lines of how a reductionist would render the PS argument.[8]

We have just witnessed how the reductionist version of the argument will likely rely on a premise that extrinsic denominations are not genuine predicate concepts. Indeed, this premise is arguably the most crucial one for the reductionist argument. For if it is denied and extrinsic denominations are permitted as predicate concepts, it will be difficult to avoid the result that extrinsic denominations are properties of things, which is the central thrust of my non-reductionist reading of the argument. The textual plausibility of this premise thus bears looking at. Such a look will reveal that the premise is unlikely to have been something that Leibniz endorsed.

IV. Are Extrinsic Denominations Genuine Predicate Concepts?

I believe there are very solid textual reasons for thinking that Leibniz regarded extrinsic denominations as genuine predicate concepts and that PS is thus applicable to propositions involving them. First of all, we have seen how in the *Primary Truths*, only two paragraphs prior to making his PS argument, Leibniz seems to state explicitly that PS is applicable to propositions involving extrinsic denominations. Are we to believe that two paragraphs following this statement he then sets forth an argument that relies on a denial of it as an *unstated* premise? It would be confusing, to say the least, for Leibniz to write that PS is the nature of truth for every affirmative proposition, "universal or particular, necessary or contingent, *and in the case of both an intrinsic and an extrinsic denomination,*" and then almost immediately thereafter write an argument in which it is left to the reader to supply the premise that PS is not applicable to propositions involving extrinsic denominations. A reductionist may respond to this by saying that, even though Leibniz seems to say that PS is applicable to such propositions, he believes it applies to them only *indirectly*. That is, it applies to them after and only after they have been properly reduced to propositions having only intrinsic denominations as predicates. PS *is* applicable to propositions with intrinsic denominations as predicates, and it is from these, according to the reductionist view, that the truth of propositions involving extrinsic denominations can be inferred. So, in this indirect sense, PS is applicable to such propositions, and that is all Leibniz is maintaining in the above quote from *Primary Truths*. Of course, the above passage does not contain even a hint of such a distinction between direct versus indirect application of PS to propositions. Leibniz simply says that PS is the criterion for the truth of *any* proposition, and then he lists all the sorts of propositions to which this criterion applies, among which are propositions involving extrinsic denominations. And he gives no indication that the criterion operates any differently in the case of propositions involving extrinsic denominations than it does with universal propositions or propositions involving intrinsic denominations. I believe, then, that it is quite reasonable to conclude that Leibniz did believe PS was straightforwardly applicable to propositions containing extrinsic denominations. And if this is true, then it is also evidence that he viewed extrinsic denominations as genuine predicate concepts that could be included in subject concepts.

The claim that extrinsic denominations are not predicate concepts, and that, as a result, PS is not applicable to propositions involving them, is textually implausible on other grounds as well. As is well-known, Leibniz employs PS to derive his doctrine of complete individual concepts, the doctrine that corresponding to each individual (possible and actual, apparently) there is a concept of that individual which contains the concepts of every predicate, necessary or contingent, past, present, and future, that could be truly asserted of that individual.[9] In the *Correspondence with Arnauld*, he says that

> when I say that the individual notion of Adam includes everything that will ever happen to him, I do not mean anything other than what all philosophers mean when they say that in true propositions the predicate is included in the subject.[10]

In more than one passage where Leibniz offers examples of the sorts of concepts that are included in complete individual concepts as a result of PS, he includes extrinsic denominations among the list. The concept of Julius Caesar includes the extrinsic denomination "destroyer of the liberty of the Romans" as a result of PS[11] and Alexander's concept contains "conqueror of Darius and Porus" for the same reason.[12]

Cover and Hawthorne reckon such texts as providing only weak support for the claim that Leibniz regarded extrinsic denominations as predicates. Such texts, they say, do present grounds for saying that some predicates are relational, but that is not what we need. Leibniz and everyone else will agree that "is the conqueror of Darius" is indeed a predicate .... What we need and don't yet have are grounds for saying that in Leibniz's final considered *lingua philosophica* they emerge as genuinely *irreducible predicates*."[13]

These remarks might possess a modest amount of force against someone who, without any additional argument, simply claims that since Leibniz calls extrinsic denominations predicates, he regarded them as properties of the denominated individual as well. After all, just because something is a predicate in a language does not necessarily mean that it expresses a property that genuinely inheres in the thing of which it is predicated.[14] However, these remarks do not appear to carry much weight against the argument that Leibniz's allowance of extrinsic denominations as predicates *together with* his predicate-in-subject principle of truth implies that he regarded extrinsic denominations as properties of the denominated individual. For if extrinsic denominations are predicates, as Cover and Hawthorne allow, then what can prevent the PS principle from applying to propositions having them as predicates, especially given Leibniz's explicit statement from *Primary Truths* that PS is the criterion of truth for propositions involving extrinsic denominations? And if the PS principle does apply to propositions having them as predicates, then how can Cover and Hawthorne prevent those denominations from being included in the denominated individual's concept (at least in the case of true propositions)?

V. Are Extrinsic Denominations the Sort of Predicates to which PS Can Apply?

They may well respond, however, that though extrinsic denominations are predicate concepts in some sense, they are not the sort of predicate concepts to which the PS principle was meant to apply. They would then, of course, have the burden of explaining—in a principled and textually well-founded way—which predicates the PS doctrine of truth applies to and which it does not. I cannot be certain how they would approach this, but, in order to keep extrinsic denominations out of complete individual concepts, they will have to alight on some way of restricting the PS principle's application to only those propositions whose predicate concepts are intrinsic denominations. Is there any textual support for such a restriction? There are certainly texts that appear to count against such a restriction, such as Leibniz's explicit statement that PS is the criterion of truth for propositions involving both intrinsic and extrinsic denominations. Nevertheless, based on claims made in their discussion, I believe Cover and Hawthorne would appeal to at least two passages to support the view that Leibniz would not apply PS to just any predicate.[15] In section 8 of the *Discourse on Metaphysics,* instead of saying that all of Alexander's predicates are included in his concept as a result of PS, Leibniz says, "*the foundation of*" and reason for all the predicates that can be truly stated of him—as, for example, that he is "the conqueror of Darius and Porus," are what is included in his concept.[16] Cover and Hawthorne take this passage to mean that what one finds in the concept of Alexander is the foundation of and reason for the extrinsic denomination <the conqueror of Darius and Porus>, not necessarily that denomination itself. Second, there is this passage from the *Correspondence with Arnauld* where Leibniz, again discussing what concepts are found in an individual concept as a result of PS, states

> For all the predicates of Adam either depend upon other predicates of the same Adam, or they do not so depend. Putting on one side, then, those which do depend on others, we have only to take together the primary predicates in order to form the complete notion of Adam, which is sufficient to make it possible to deduce from it everything which must happen to him, as far as is necessary to give an explanation of it.[17]

The point of this passage, for Cover and Hawthorne, is that the primary predicates of Adam are the foundations for all the other predicates of Adam, and they are the only predicates to be found in Adam's concept. PS does not result in complete individual concepts containing every predicate that can be truly stated of a thing. Rather, individual concepts contain only those predicates needed to infer the truth of all the others. This may seem to imply that Leibniz endorsed some sort of restriction on the sorts of predicates to which PS applies, or that he endorsed some sort of distinction between direct and indirect application of PS to propositions, with the result being that some propositions are true because the concept of the predicate is included in the concept of the subject, while others are true because they can be derived from such propositions. And, of course, Cover and Hawthorne will regard the former sort of true propositions as ones whose predicates are *intrinsic* denominations, and they will regard the latter sort of true propositions as ones whose predicates are *extrinsic* denominations.

But the above two passages provide support for such a restriction on PS's scope of application only if, when Leibniz speaks of "foundations" and "primary predicates," he has intrinsic denominations in mind. The passages themselves do not suggest the identification of "foundations" or "primary predicates" with intrinsic denominations. Reductionists may nevertheless urge such an identification on the following grounds. As discussed in chapter one, Leibniz, in other places, explicitly asserts that extrinsic denominations are founded on intrinsic denominations.[18] Of course, how such passages should be understood is a subject of deep dispute between reductionists and non-reductionists, and I shall have much more to say on this matter in chapter five. Nevertheless, if one were to assume, as Cover and Hawthorne apparently do, that Leibniz has roughly the same thing in mind in those passages that he does in those from the preceding paragraph, then one could take "foundations" to represent intrinsic denominations. Furthermore, in the PS argument for NPE itself, Leibniz concludes with more than just the words, "there are no purely extrinsic denominations," but with the more detailed claim that "there are no purely extrinsic denominations, *which have no foundation in the thing denominated.*" In the PS argument for NPE, Leibniz wants to show that the PS principle implies that extrinsic denominations have a foundation in the denominated thing. Again, if we assume that this conclusion is just another way of asserting that extrinsic denominations are founded on intrinsic denominations, we would have good grounds for restricting the PS principle's applicability to propositions having intrinsic denominations as predicates, and thus for reconstructing the PS argument for NPE in something like the reductionist manner described earlier. What we now must consider, then, is whether it is plausible to understand Leibniz's use of "foundation" in the conclusion of the PS argument for NPE, and in the two passages above, as a reference to intrinsic denominations. As I shall argue in the next section, such a construal of Leibnizian foundations in these contexts is highly doubtful. Moreover, once a proper understanding of such foundations is achieved, it will become clear that the above passages actually provide striking support for the reading of NPE I propose.

VI. On Leibniz's Use of the Term "Foundation" in the Context of his PS Principle of Truth

Leibniz frequently employs the term "foundation" in connection with his PS notion of truth. In the *Correspondence with Arnauld* he says,

> In every affirmative true proposition, necessary or contingent, universal or singular, the notion of the predicate is contained in some way in that of the subject .... Now I ask no more connection here than that which exists *a parte rei* between the terms of a true proposition; and it is in this sense only that I say that the individual substance includes all its events and all its denominations ... since there must always be some foundation of the connexion of the terms of a proposition, which foundation must lie in their notions.[19]

As C.D. Broad and others have observed, the passage indicates that the foundation of the connection of the terms of a true proposition just is that the concept of the predicate is in the concept of the subject.[20] As the passage explains, the concept of an individual substance must contain everything that can be truly stated of that substance (i.e., it must be a complete individual concept); otherwise, there could be a *true* proposition about that substance whose predicate concept was not included in its subject concept, which would violate the PS doctrine of truth. The connection between the terms of such a proposition would lack the requisite foundation for truth under the PS criterion. Said in another way, a predicate concept has a foundation in the subject concept just in case it is included in that subject concept.

This understanding of foundations in PS contexts is corroborated by Leibniz's explicit connection of such foundations for truth with what he calls the "reason" for a proposition and also the "*a priori* proof" of a proposition. In an important essay entitled *The Nature of Truth* he says,

> A true proposition is one whose predicate is contained in its subject, or, more generally whose consequent is contained in its antecedent, and it is therefore necessary that there should be some connection between the notions of the terms, i.e. that there should be an objective foundation from which the reason for the proposition can be given, or an *a priori* proof can be found.[21]

Let us first examine the connection of the foundation for the truth of a proposition with the reason for a proposition. In addition to the preceding passage, the two passages cited earlier, those that Cover and Hawthorne claim have such a strong reductionist flavor, link the notion of a foundation with the notion of giving a reason. The quote from *Discourse* section 8 asserts that Alexander's individual concept contains *both* "the foundation of *and reason for* all the predicates which can truly be stated of him." Additionally, in the passage from the Leibniz-Arnauld Correspondence, Leibniz claims that primary predicates found in Adam's concept "make it possible to deduce from it everything which must happen to him, *as far as is necessary to give an explanation of it.*" It is exceedingly clear from these passages that whatever serves as the foundation of a truth must also provide a reason for the truth. And what, for Leibniz, provides the reason for a truth? A true proposition has a reason just in case its predicate concept is included in its subject concept.

> The fundamental principle of reasoning is that there is nothing without a reason; or, to explain the matter more distinctly, that there is no truth for which a reason does not subsist. The reason for a truth consists in the connection of the predicate with the subject, that is, that the predicate is in the subject.[22]

Thus, if the reason for a truth is that its predicate concept is included in its subject concept *and* if the reason for a truth is also the foundation for that truth, then the foundation of a truth is that its predicate concept is in its subject concept.

The earlier quote from *The Nature of Truth* also indicates that the foundation of a truth provides what Leibniz terms as an *a priori* proof of the truth. According to Leibniz, an a priori proof of a proposition amounts to a demonstration that the proposition is an identical one. An identical proposition is, roughly, a proposition that states a term of itself.[23] As examples of such Leibniz offers, "a man is a man" and "a white man is white."[24] But, for Leibniz, *every* true proposition is an identical one. Some true propositions are identical on their faces, but others have to be shown to be identical by means of an *a priori* proof. In *Primary Truths*, Leibniz explains that

> Primary truths [i.e., identical truths] are those which either state a term of itself or deny an opposite of its opposite. For example, 'A is A', or 'A is not not-A'.... All other truths are reduced to primary truths by the aid of definitions—i.e., by the analysis of notions; and this constitutes a priori proof, independent of experience.[25]

The process of providing an a priori proof for a proposition, that is, the process of showing the proposition to be identical, is carried out, says Leibniz, through the analysis of notions or by the aid of definitions. The idea here is that in the covertly identical propositions, if one substitutes definitions for defined terms (perhaps again and again) one will eventually reduce the proposition to an overtly identical one.[26] Consider Leibniz's analysis of the proposition, "Nine is a square." This is not an overtly identical proposition. Yet since it is a true proposition, it must ultimately be an identical proposition and this can be demonstrated via an *a priori* proof. Thus, Leibniz says, "nine is three times three, which is three multiplied by three, which is a number multiplied by itself, which is a square."[27] We are then left with the proposition, "A square (plus whatever other properties belong to the number nine) is a square," which is straightforwardly identical.

Leibniz's doctrine that every true proposition is identical is inextricably bound with his PS doctrine of truth. According to PS, a proposition is true if and only if the concept of the predicate is included in the concept of the subject. But a predicate concept is included in a subject concept if and only if the proposition is an identical one or reduces to an identical one by means of an *a priori* demonstration. In *Primary Truths*, we find

> The predicate or consequent, therefore, is always in the subject or antecedent, and this constitutes the nature of truth in general, or, the connection between the terms of a proposition, as Aristotle also has observed. In identities this connection and inclusion of the predicate in the subject is express, whereas in all other truths it is implicit and must be shown through the analysis of notions, in which *a priori* demonstration consists.[28]

An identical proposition is one that states a term of itself, a proposition of the form "A is A" or "ABC is A." But a true proposition is one whose predicate concept is already in its subject concept, and so a true proposition is quite literally one that states a term of itself. An acceptance of the PS doctrine of truth and the claim that every true proposition is identical thus go hand in hand.

Furthermore, Leibniz's doctrine that every true proposition is identical or has an *a priori* proof is inseparably joined to his view that there is a reason for every true proposition. That is, there is a reason for a proposition just in case the proposition has an *a priori* proof. In *An Introduction to a Secret Encyclopedia*, Leibniz declares,

> that proposition is true which is identical or is reducible to identical propositions; that is, which can be demonstrated *a priori*, or, the connection of whose predicate with its subject can be exhibited in such a way that its reason always appears. And indeed, nothing at all happens without some reason, i.e. there is no proposition except identical ones, in which the connection between subject and predicate cannot be displayed distinctly.[29]

Given this equivalence between a proposition being identical and a proposition having a reason, it is no wonder that in the earlier quoted passage from *The Nature of Truth* Leibniz indicates that the *foundation* for a truth provides both the reason for the truth and an *a priori* proof of it. But, as we have seen, a true proposition has a reason just in case its predicate is included in its subject, and a proposition is identical, or has an *a priori* proof, just in case its predicate is included in its subject. It is quite plausible, then, to regard the foundation of a true proposition, or, as Leibniz phrases it, the foundation of the connection of the terms of a true proposition, as being that the proposition's predicate is included in its subject.

With this understanding of a Leibnizian foundation before us, we can now consider whether intrinsic denominations are plausibly regarded as the foundation Leibniz has in mind for propositions involving extrinsic denominations. When Cover and Hawthorne cite the earlier quoted passages from the *Discourse* and the *Correspondence with Arnauld* concerning the predicates that are found in the concepts of Alexander and Adam (respectively), they claim that the passages display a strong reductionist tone and support the view that intrinsic denominations are the foundations Leibniz has in view. Yet both of these passages, as mentioned above, strongly imply that the foundation of a proposition is also what furnishes the reason for the proposition. The issue concerning whether intrinsic denominations can function as foundations for extrinsic denominations can therefore be framed in the following way: can intrinsic denominations provide reasons for propositions that ascribe an extrinsic denomination to a subject? Given the understanding of reasons for propositions discussed above, intrinsic denominations clearly cannot perform such a function.

Leibniz states in the *Discourse* that Alexander's concept contains the foundation of and reason for the extrinsic denomination <the conqueror of Darius and Porus>. I believe at least two assertions are contained in this claim:

(10) The proposition "Alexander is the conqueror of Darius and Porus" has a reason.

(11) The reason for this proposition is to be found in Alexander's complete individual concept.

And if Leibniz accepts (10) and (11), he cannot have regarded intrinsic denominations as the foundation. As we have seen, a proposition has a reason just in case it is an identical proposition or admits of an *a priori* proof. If the proposition "Alexander is the conqueror of Darius and Porus" is to have a reason, then it must be an identical proposition, a proposition that states a term of itself. That is, in order for the proposition to have a reason, it must be of the form "A is A" or "ABC is B." Now, according to reductionists, complete individual concepts contain only intrinsic denominations. It would seem, then, that the only type of denominations to be found in the subject concept of this proposition is intrinsic denominations of Alexander. But if Alexander's concept includes only his intrinsic denominations, then no proposition having his concept as its subject and an extrinsic denomination as its predicate could seemingly ever be identical. The extrinsic denomination <conqueror of Darius and Porus> could never be identical to any subset of Alexander's *intrinsic* denominations. But if the proposition is not identical, then it has no reason. Yet Leibniz says that Alexander's concept contains the foundation of and reason for *all* the predicates that can be truly stated of him, including extrinsic denominations. Intrinsic denominations, therefore, simply do not suffice as a foundation for such propositions.

One fairly predictable reductionist response is that Leibniz did not intend the requirements of giving a reason and an *a priori* proof to apply directly to propositions having extrinsic denominations as predicates. Reductionists might agree that the PS principle is tightly connected to these requirements, as I have been arguing. But just as they do not allow PS to apply directly to propositions having extrinsic denominations as predicates (that is, PS applies directly only to propositions whose predicates are intrinsic denominations, and it is from these that the truth of propositions whose predicates are extrinsic denominations as predicates can be inferred), they will not allow these requirements to apply directly to such propositions. Propositions having intrinsic denominations as predicates, the ones to which the propositions having extrinsic denominations reduce, have reasons and are identical. And, in this *indirect* sense, propositions having extrinsic denominations as predicates have reasons and are identical. Leibniz does not demand that propositions whose predicates are extrinsic denominations be identical; he only requires that the propositions to which these reduce be identical. But there are simply no textual grounds for this response. Leibniz nowhere suggests that the requirements of giving a reason and an *a priori* proof operate differently on propositions involving extrinsic denominations than they do on propositions involving intrinsic denominations. Further, this sort of move is beginning to look just a bit *ad hoc*. When confronted with the seemingly clear implication of the PS principle that propositions having extrinsic denominations are true because their predicates are in their subjects, reductionists claim that PS does not apply directly to such propositions. In support of this, they offer certain passages where Leibniz speaks of complete individual concepts containing only the predicates that serve as the foundations for all the rest. But when it is shown that Leibniz regards the foundations as providing both for the reasons and the identical nature of these propositions, and that intrinsic denominations cannot furnish either, reductionists invent yet another textually unfounded distinction between direct versus indirect application of the reason and identicality requirements. I cannot see any reason why anyone who was not already committed to reductionism should find any of this even mildly persuasive.

If intrinsic denominations do not provide the foundation, then what would have to be included in Alexander's concept in order for it to contain the reason for "Alexander is the conqueror of Darius and Porus"? It would seem that nothing less than the extrinsic denomination <the conqueror of Darius and Porus> would suffice. In order for a proposition to be identical, and thus have a reason, the predicate has to be in the subject. And since whatever provides the reason for a proposition is also the foundation for it, it must be that the foundation of "Alexander is the conqueror of Darius and Porus" is that the extrinsic denomination <conqueror of Darius and Porus> is included in Alexander's concept. The foundation of and reason for a predicate's being truly stateable of a subject is that the predicate is included in the subject.

But this, if true, would seem to raise a problem. For it appears that every last predicate that can be truly stated of Alexander must be in his concept in order to guarantee that every true proposition having Alexander's concept as subject will have a reason. What of Leibniz's assertion that complete individual concepts contain only an individual's "primary predicates" from which all the other (non-primary) predicates follow? This was the point of the earlier quoted passage from the Leibniz-Arnauld correspondence concerning the predicates that reside in Adam's concept. Some of the predicates that are truly stateable of Adam are not, strictly speaking, in his concept; rather, they follow from those predicates that are in his concept. But if this is so, will every true proposition concerning Adam still be identical? To see why one might think this is a problem, consider a proposition that truly ascribes some non-primary predicate, P, to Adam. To have a reason, the proposition "Adam is P" must be identical. But P, being non-primary, would seem not to be included in Adam's concept, and so how could "Adam is P" be identical? As things look on their face, it is difficult to see how the proposition could be reduced to one having the form "ABC . . . P . . . is P," if P is not in Adam's concept.

Once we understand what Leibniz means by "primary predicates" and also how he understands the logical relationship between primary predicates and non-primary ones, this problem quickly disappears, however. Let it be clear from the outset that Leibniz does *not* have intrinsic denominations in mind when he speaks of primary predicates. For, as the Leibniz-Arnauld passage states, the primary predicates provide an explanation (i.e., a reason) for everything that can be stated of Adam, and as we have seen, intrinsic denominations cannot provide a reason for the extrinsic denominations that are true of an individual. So, another understanding of primary predicates must be sought. The passage itself states that some of Adam's predicates depend on other predicates being true of Adam, while other of Adam's predicates do not depend on others. Leibniz labels the latter category of Adam's predicates as the primary predicates and the former category as non-primary predicates. This way of distinguishing primary from non-primary predicates is strongly reminiscent of the way Leibniz distinguishes simple concepts from non-simple or complex ones. For this reason, I believe that, for Leibniz, the primary predicates of a thing are the simple concepts under which that thing falls.[30] According to Leibniz, concepts come in two varieties: simple and complex. Simple, or, as Leibniz sometimes calls them, primary or primitive, concepts are concepts which are conceived through themselves and cannot be analyzed into other concepts.[31] Complex or derivative concepts are conceived through other concepts and can be analyzed into other concepts. Complex concepts are formed, roughly, either by conjoining simple concepts together or by negation.[32] In *Of Universal Synthesis and Analysis*, Leibniz states that, "all derivative concepts arise from a combination of primitive ones, and those which are composite in a higher degree arise from a combination of composite concepts."[33] The complex concept <human>, for example, is formed by combining the concepts <rational> and <animal>, and of course, the concepts <rational> and <animal> are themselves complex and can be analyzed into simpler concepts. Thus I believe the sense in which non-primary predicates depend on the primary ones is that the non-primary ones are formed by combining the primary ones and that the non-primary ones can be analyzed into primary ones.

Such an understanding of primary predicates and their logical relationship to non-primary ones resolves the above difficulty of how individual concepts can contain only primitive predicates and yet still provide a reason for every predicate that can be truly stated of the individual falling under that concept. Recall that when Leibniz states his PS principle of truth, he says that there are two ways a predicate can be included in its subject: "expressly in the case of primitive or identical truths . . . but implicitly in the case of all the rest. This implicit inclusion is shown by the analysis of terms, by substituting for one another definitions and what is defined."[34] Given that individual concepts contain only primary predicates, that is, simple concepts, then any proposition whose subject concept is a complete individual concept and whose predicate is a primitive concept will be explicitly identical. But propositions that truly ascribe a non-primary predicate to such a subject are implicitly identical and are shown to be identical by means of an *a priori* proof.[35] In other words, their predicates are implicitly included in their subjects. Yet both types of propositions are ultimately identical and so have a reason. The predicate concept <a human> is true of Adam, but it is not included in his concept as such; it is implicitly included. For <a human> is analyzed into <a rational animal>, which is further analyzed into simpler concepts, down to the level of primitive concepts.[36] And it is the primitive concepts out of which <a human> is formed that are expressly included in Adam's concept. Yet because the primitive concepts that define what being human is are included in Adam's concept, it is quite appropriate to speak of the predicate <a human> as being included (implicitly) in his concept and of the proposition "Adam is a human" as being identical.

It bears pointing out that extrinsic denominations are also complex concepts that are formed by combining simple ones.[37] The extrinsic denomination <the conqueror of Darius and Porus> is a complex concept, but it is obviously not formed by combining Alexander's primitve *intrinsic* denominations. And this is why, as has been shown, intrinsic denominations cannot provide a "foundation of and reason for" extrinsic denominations. For if Alexander's concept contains only his primitive intrinsic denominations, then the proposition "Alexander is the conqueror of Darius and Porus" will not be identical. Rather, <the conqueror of Darius and Porus> is comprised of the primitive concepts out of which its components—i.e., <conqueror>, <Darius>, <Porus>, etc.—are formed. And so long as the composite of primitive concepts comprising <the conqueror of Darius and Porus> is in Alexander's concept, the proposition "Alexander is the conqueror of Darius and Porus" will be identical.[38]

VII. The PS Argument for NPE Revisited

The passages stating that Alexander's and Adam's concepts contain the foundations of all the predicates that are truly stateable of them were, recall, originally put forth, on behalf of reductionists, to support a restriction on the sorts of predicates to which the PS principle could apply. The only predicates that can enter individual concepts as a result of PS are the ones that are the foundations for the rest. Cover and Hawthorne assume that intrinsic denominations are the foundation Leibniz has in mind, and thus the only sort of predicates that PS applies to and that appear in complete individual concepts are intrinsic denominations. Yet once we realize that foundations must also provide reasons for propositions, we see that intrinsic denominations simply cannot provide the necessary foundation. Therefore, the passages concerning

Alexander's and Adam's individual concepts do not support the claim that the PS principle only applies to propositions having intrinsic denominations as predicates. And this, in turn, means that any reductionist reconstruction of the PS argument for NPE that relies upon this restriction of PS remains as doubtful as ever. In fact, once a proper understanding of "foundation" and "primary predicate" is gained, the passages actually suggest quite the contrary. That is, once we realize that foundations and primary predicates must provide a reason for the predicates that are truly stateable of a thing, the passages strongly imply that extrinsic denominations must be included in the concepts of what they denominate.

As shown earlier, for Leibniz, the foundation of a true proposition is that its predicate is included in its subject, or a predicate has a foundation in a subject just in case it is included in that subject. This is the only understanding of a foundation that can do the work of providing a reason for true propositions or of allowing for them to be identical. This understanding of a Leibnizian foundation permits us to see even more clearly why the interpretation of NPE contained in (6) is the conclusion Leibniz intends to draw in the PS argument for NPE. *Primary Truths* begins with Leibniz claiming that all truths are identical or can be reduced to identities "by the aid of definitions— i.e. by the analysis of notions; and this constitutes *a priori* proof." He then says that because of this, the predicate must be in the subject. The only way that every true proposition can state a term of itself (i.e., be identical) is if the term stated of the subject is already included in the subject of which it is stated. Immediately thereafter, Leibniz then says the following:

> In identities this connection and inclusion of the predicate in the subject is express, whereas in all other truths it is implicit and must be shown through the analysis of notions, in which a priori demonstration consists.
> But this is true in the case of every affirmative truth, universal or particular, necessary or contingent, *and in the case of both an intrinsic and an extrinsic denomination.*[39]

This passage appears to assert quite plainly that propositions having extrinsic denominations as predicates, no less than propositions whose predicates are intrinsic denominations, are identical and can be shown so by means of an *a priori* proof. And such a showing demonstrates that the extrinsic denomination is included in the concept of the denominated thing. Reductionists will undoubtedly reply that when Leibniz says that extrinsic denominations are included in the concept of the denominated individual and that this can be shown by means of an *a priori* proof, what he means is that the intrinsic denominations that provide the foundation for the extrinsic denomination are what is included. But we can now see that this reading of Leibniz is simply untenable. First, it does not really make any sense as a reading of the passage just quoted. If that is what Leibniz meant, then why does he say "and in the case of both an intrinsic and an extrinsic denomination," as though both were in the denominated thing in the same way? Secondly, as we have seen, intrinsic denominations cannot furnish an *a priori* proof for propositions whose predicates are extrinsic denominations. I believe Leibniz understood the implications of his own doctrine of truth and its connections to his notions of *a priori* proof and the reason for a proposition. Thus, when he says that extrinsic denominations are included in the concept of the denominated individual and that this is shown by means of an *a priori* proof, he means just that. He simply cannot mean what reductionists say he means.

Following the passage just quoted, Leibniz says that because of that doctrine of truth, "there follow many things of great importance." The first of which is that every truth has a reason, which he equates with every truth being identical and with every truth having an *a priori* proof.[40]

And then, a paragraph later, he sets forth the PS argument for NPE as yet another consequence of his doctrine of truth.

> It also follows that there are no purely extrinsic denominations, which have no foundation in the thing denominated. For the notion of the subject must involve the notion of the predicate.

The first sentence of the quote suggests that a purely extrinsic denomination is one that has no foundation in the thing denominated. As mentioned earlier, many reductionists eagerly use this sentence as a proof text of their view. Now, I agree that the sentence does imply that purely extrinsic denominations are denominations which lack a foundation in the denominated thing. However, once a correct understanding of "foundation" is acquired, the sentence becomes a proof text for *my* reading of NPE. A denomination that has no foundation in the denominated thing is one that is not included in the denominated thing. And why can there not be any of those? For precisely the reason Leibniz gives: "the notion of the subject must involve the notion of the predicate." NPE, when read as (6), is precisely the claim that there are no extrinsic denominations that are not included in what they denominate. Given all that Leibniz says in the paragraphs preceding the PS argument for NPE, and in the PS argument itself, it is difficult to imagine an interpretation of NPE that could better serve as the result here.

This construction of the PS argument for NPE is also strikingly corroborated by the following passage from the *Correspondence with Arnauld* in which Leibniz, immediately after stating the PS principle of truth, says,

> Now I ask no more connection here than that which exists *a parte rei* between the terms of a true proposition; and it is in this sense only that I say that the individual substance includes all its events and all its denominations, *even those*

which are commonly called extrinsic (that is they belong to it only by virtue of the general interconnection of things and because it expresses the whole universe in its own way) *since there must always be some foundation of the connection of the terms of a proposition, which foundation must lie in their notions.*[41]

This passage straightforwardly asserts that because of the PS principle, individual concepts must include extrinsic denominations, since there must be a foundation for the connection of the terms of a true proposition. So, in *Primary Truths*, when Leibniz says that because of the PS principle, there are no purely extrinsic denominations, which have no foundation in the denominated thing, he can well be understood as trying to prove that extrinsic denominations are included in what they denominate. Their inclusion in the concept of what they denominate is what provides them with a foundation, as the Leibniz-Arnauld passage indicates.

VI. A Further Difficulty for Reductionism

Further doubts arise concerning the reductionist interpretation of NPE when we consider how one might infer (9)—the claim that as often as the denomination of a thing is changed, there is a change in the thing itself—from the reductionist NPE claim. Reductionist NPE maintains that whatever extrinsic denominations are true of a thing can be inferred from the intrinsic denominations of that thing and the intrinsic denominations of other things. Can this claim guarantee that as often as a change occurs in the denomination of a thing, there will be a change in the thing itself? In an earlier example involving the heights of Andrew and Bernard, we had it that Andrew is taller than Bernard. Suppose, though, that Bernard is ten years older than Andrew. This would mean that for many years after Andrew was born, Bernard was taller than Andrew; that is, the extrinsic denomination <taller than Andrew> truly denominated Bernard at one point. But at some point in Andrew's teen years, he overtakes Bernard in respect of height. At that point, <taller than Andrew> ceases to apply to Bernard— a change has occurred in one of his extrinsic denominations. So, given (9), we should expect to find a change in Bernard, a change that we can infer as a result of the reductionist NPE assertion being true. Presumably, it is not the height of Bernard that has changed, since he is by now in his mid to late twenties. Of course, one of Andrew's extrinsic denominations has changed as well. The extrinsic denomination <taller than Bernard> is now true of him, and that change in his extrinsic denominations has been accompanied by a change in him (i.e., his height). But what has changed in Bernard? Merely knowing that <shorter than Andrew> (which is the extrinsic denomination that is now true of Bernard) can be inferred form intrinsic denominations of Andrew and Bernard does not, by itself, imply that something in Bernard (i.e., one of his intrinsic denominations) has changed. It would seem, then, that the reductionist needs to furnish another premise or premises in order to get to (9). Under my interpretation of NPE, as given by (6), the inference to (9) from NPE was immediate. For (6), if true, means that extrinsic denominations are properties included in the concepts of things. So, if an extrinsic denomination of a thing is changed there will be a change in the thing itself (or, better, in the thing's concept, and, consequently, in the thing itself), since the change of extrinsic denomination *itself* is what has changed in the thing. The reductionist, however, apparently cannot move from his version of NPE to (9) as easily.

As before, since no reductionist interpreter of whom I am aware has attempted to fill in the inference from NPE to (9), I can only offer what I believe to be the candidates for the missing premise a reductionist would be most likely to choose. The goal, of course, is to alight on a premise that can be plausibly regarded as something Leibniz could have had in mind (but for whatever reason chose not to state) when he penned this argument. One reasonable candidate is Leibniz's well-known claim that

(12) A change in one substance entails a change in every other.[42]

This would certainly do the trick in the above case. There was no difficulty in seeing what had changed in Andrew when the extrinsic denomination <taller than Bernard> became true of him: his height increased. And if a change in one thing entails a change in every other, then it follows that Bernard has changed as well. This does not tell us *what* has changed in Bernard, but if <taller than Andrew> no longer applies to Bernard as a result of a change in Andrew, then, by (12), Bernard has changed. Another natural choice for the missing link between NPE and (9) is Leibniz's doctrine that every substance expresses the entire universe. This claim is typically understood as

(13) By examining the properties of any single monad at a given moment in time a sufficiently discerning mind can determine the past, present and future properties of all other monads.[43]

If a change in an extrinsic denomination of Bernard has come about as a result of a change in Andrew's intrinsic denominations (presumably, his height), then it would seem that, given (13), a change must have occurred in Bernard's properties as well so that they can now express Andrew's new height.[44] Beyond (12) and (13), there appear to be no other plausible candidates to fill the gap here.

Now, there are two ways that (12) or (13) could fit into the argument for (9). They could be viewed as consequences of NPE themselves that are then deployed to reach (9), or they could be regarded as claims that stand independently of NPE and which are implicitly added to NPE here to infer (9). The latter alternative is rather implausible, for if that was what Leibniz had in mind, then the NPE claim would be superfluous to the proof of (9). Both of (12) and (13) are strong enough by themselves to infer (9) without the help of the reductionist version of NPE. It is rather unlikely that Leibniz in attempting to derive (9) from NPE employed an unstated premise which by itself would yield (9). Any plausible reconstruction of Leibniz's thinking here must surely find a way to make NPE vital to the establishment of (9).

It thus appears that we should view one of (12) or (13) as consequences of NPE that Leibniz implicitly uses to infer (13). Setting aside, for the moment, the issue of whether there is any plausible way to obtain either of these claims from reductionist NPE, this alternative is subject to serious difficulty as well. In *Primary Truths*, it is only *after* proving (9) that Leibniz explicitly derives both (12) and (13), and so it seems unlikely that he would have been employing them as unstated intermediate inferences to prove (9). For instance, with regard to (13), he explicitly employs NPE as a premise for (13).[45] Why does he wait to prove (13) until after he proves (9) if he intends (13) to be a premise for (9)? He could have so easily made the argument he made for (13) first and then proven (9). And as further evidence against (12)'s suitability as the missing link, there is this passage in which Leibniz argues from PS to NPE to (9), and then to (12):

> That all existing things have this intercourse with each other can be proved ... from the fact that ... there are no extrinsic denominations and no one becomes a widower in India by the death of his wife in Europe unless a real change occurs in him. For every predicate is in fact contained in the nature of the subject.[46]

The claim that, "no one becomes a widower in India by the death of his wife in Europe unless a real change occurs in him," is simply a way of stating (9) in a particularized way. Leibniz could not very well have been employing (12) to prove (9) and then (9) to prove (12).

However, if NPE is understood in the manner of (6), the argument proceeds in seamless, linear fashion from PS to NPE to (9). This progression fits the flow that exists within *Primary Truths* itself, and does so far better than the sequence that the reductionist must use.[47]

Chapter Three

Extrinsic Denominations and Where Accidents Are Allowed to Put Their Feet

I. Introduction

Leibniz's doctrine of individual accidents asserts that an accident cannot inhere in more than one substance. As discussed in chapter one, adherence to this doctrine leads Leibniz to reject relations simpliciter as accidents. A fundamental tenet of my account of Leibniz's views on relations is that though Leibniz does not permit relations simpliciter to serve as accidents, he does believe relational accidents are genuine accidents. Cover and Hawthorne have articulated a novel objection to this view. They claim (or at least they seem to claim) that the allowance of relational accidents would violate the doctrine of individual accidents just as much as the allowance of relations simpliciter as accidents would. The primary goal of this chapter is to rebut this charge. In section II, I attempt to clarify what their objection is. Crucial to their argument is the assumption that individuals are constituents of relational accidents. For example, the relational accident "lover of Helen" contains the individual Helen as one of its constituents. Cover and Hawthorne provide no explanation of what it means for Helen to be a constituent of "lover of Helen," and thus it is difficult to evaluate their assumption that she is. To remedy this, I move the discussion from the realm of relational accidents into the realm of their conceptual counterparts—the realm of extrinsic denominations. I demonstrate that complete individual concepts are not included in extrinsic denominations, and thus there is no reason to believe that Leibniz would regard individuals as constituents of relational accidents. The showing that individual concepts are not included in extrinsic denominations requires a brief foray into Leibniz's logic of concepts and concept-inclusion, and this foray occupies much of section III. However, that individual concepts are not included in extrinsic denominations brings to light a puzzle concerning the conceptual structure of extrinsic denominations and Leibniz's logic of concepts. In the last section, then, I consider the conceptual structure of extrinsic denominations (as well as certain types of intrinsic denominations) and show that they are not expressible in Leibniz's logic of concepts.

This result is not in any way a consequence of maintaining that extrinsic denominations are properties (or that relational accidents are genuine accidents); rather it reflects a general inadequacy of Leibniz's logic of concepts.

II. The Objection

Cover and Hawthorne formulate their objection as follows:

> If the final story of Leibniz's groundfloor metaphysics includes relational facts about the substances David, Socrates and Paris falling under irreducibly relational concepts or properties, then there must be in those substances individual accidents that essentially have, respectively, Solomon and Theatetus and Helen (or their haecceitistic Proxies) as constituents. Now whatever *that* might amount to, it sounds odd coming from Leibniz: are we to believe that he rejects accidents with one leg in one substance, the other in another, but welcomes accidents with one leg in one substance and a full-nelson hug around another?[1]

Their basic charge appears to be that allowing relational accidents to be genuine accidents would violate Leibniz's doctrine of individual accidents every bit as much as it would to allow relations simpliciter as accidents. A fairly significant ambiguity exists in the argument, though. It is not clear whether they believe the relational accident as a whole would inhere in more than substance, or whether only one of the constituent parts of the accident would be in more than one substance. Consider the relational accident "father of Solomon." Is it that "father of Solomon" becomes an accident of both David and Solomon if we permit relational accidents, or is it just Solomon (the individual), which Cover and Hawthorne claim is a constituent of the accident, that inheres in both David and Solomon? I am genuinely uncertain as to which reading is correct. Nevertheless, as will be shown, on neither reading does their objection show that the admission of relational accidents violates the doctrine of individual accidents.

According to the first reading of Cover and Hawthorne's argument, if relational accidents are allowed, the whole relational accident "father of Solomon" will have a leg in David and a full-nelson hug around Solomon. The sense in which "father of Solomon" has a leg in David (if we allow relational accidents) is simply that it inheres in David—it would be one of David's accidents. But how does the accident get a leg in Solomon? The answer would seem to lie in their claim that Solomon, the individual, is a constituent of "father or Solomon." It is not at all clear what it means to regard Solomon as a constituent of an accident, but, at a minimum, such a claim involves Solomon being part of the very make-up of the accident. The accident somehow contains Solomon within itself. And it is just this sense, under the first reading of Cover and Hawthorne, that "father of Solomon" gains a full-nelson hug around

Solomon. Now when Cover and Hawthorne ask how we are to believe that Leibniz rejects accidents with one leg in one substance and one leg in another but welcomes accidents with a leg in one substance and a full-nelson hug around another, they sound as though they believe permitting relational accidents results in a particularly egregious violation of the doctrine of individual accidents. It is difficult to take such a statement in any other way. The problem with such a claim, however, is that "father of Solomon," even if it is a genuine accident of David, is simply not an accident of Solomon. I do not see how it can be, let alone how that would result from its being an accident of David. And the point about Solomon being contained in the accident as one of its constituents does not help either. Suppose that Solomon is contained in the accident. His relationship to that accident is something like that of part to whole. That he is such a constituent of "father of Solomon" surely does not mean that "father of Solomon" is an accident of *his*. In order to transgress the doctrine of individual accidents, "father of Solomon" must be an accident of both David and Solomon. If we allow relational accidents, then it will be an accident of David, but there is no sensible way of regarding it as an accident of Solomon, and so permitting it to be an accident of David does not run afoul of the doctrine of individual accidents. Thus, if Cover and Hawthorne's point was that allowing relational accidents leads to those same relational accidents being in more that one substance, then their objection completely fails.[2]

Perhaps Cover and Howthorne's point is not that "father of Solomon" has a leg in both David and Solomon, but rather that its constituent, Solomon, somehow becomes an accident of both David and Solomon. That is, perhaps their argument relies on the following:

(14) If C is a constituent of an accident A and A is an accident of a substance S, then C is an accident of S.

Thus if Solomon is a constituent of "father of Solomon" and "father of Solomon" is an accident of David, then Solomon is also an accident of David. Solomon would then have a leg in David and a full-nelson hug around *himself*. It is somewhat strange to think of Solomon as an accident in this way, but if we can regard him thusly, then we would seem to have a clear violation of the doctrine of individual accidents. Solomon is being predicated of David by virtue of being a constituent of one of David's accidents, and he can, I suppose, also be said of himself. Moreover, an analogous result would seem to hold true at the level of concepts. For Leibniz, complete individual concepts are the conceptual counterparts of individuals and extrinsic denominations are the conceptual counterparts of relational accidents. Now, concept-inclusion is a transitive relation.[3] So, if the complete individual concept <Solomon> is included in <father of Solomon> and <father of Solomon> is included in <David>, then <Solomon> is included in <David>. And as, for Leibniz, every concept is included in itself, <Solomon> is included in <Solomon>.[4] Thus, the concept <Solomon> is, it would appear, included in both <David> and <Solomon>.[5]

This problem is further aggravated by the fact that Leibniz held to what might be termed an Aristotelian view of substance. Leibniz says, "when several predicates are attributed to one and the same subject, and this subject is not attributed to any other, one calls this subject an individual substance."[6] Leibniz, then, would almost certainly not allow the predication of Solomon to David that seems to result here.

I am not certain that Solomon, in his alleged role of constituent of the accident "father of Solomon," is what Cover and Hawthorne regard as the accident that has a leg in David and a full-nelson hug around Solomon, but it is surely a more promising alternative than the whole accident "father of Solomon." I will assume from here on, then, that this is the objection Cover and Hawthorne intend.

Cover and Hawthorne's objection (on either reading) crucially depends on the claim that Solomon is a constituent of the accident "father of Solomon." What does it mean to regard Solomon, the individual, as a constituent of an accident? It is not at all clear what this might involve, and Cover and Hawthorne, unfortunately, are completely silent on the matter. To speak of Solomon as a *constituent* of "father of Solomon" suggests, albeit vaguely, that "father of Solomon" is constructed by combining Solomon with certain other ingredients (a relation, perhaps?). Solomon himself is somehow contained within the accident. But it is very difficult to understand how an accident could contain a substance within itself. Of course, Cover and Hawthorne might well assert that whatever strangeness surrounds such a notion is so much the worse for the prospects of relational accidents. That is, if in order to form relational accidents, substances must be constituents of those accidents, then the metaphysical peculiarity of that is yet another reason why we should not countenance such accidents. But must an accident contain an individual as a *constituent* in order to be a relational accident? Clearly, relational accidents, like "father of Solomon," involve individuals in *some* way, but why must that involvement be that such accidents contain individuals as constituents? It seems at least possible, and even likely, that individuals are related to relational accidents in some way other that that of constituent to thing constituted, or part to whole, or contained to container. I will not attempt to develop an affirmative account of this here. I merely wish to suggest that it is far from obvious that relational accidents must possess individuals as constituents in order to be relational accidents. And if individuals are not constituents of relational accidents, then the antecedent conditions set in (14) are not met, and then there is no reason to suppose that those individuals become accidents in more than one substance.

This response, however, does not help if we move from the level of substances and relational accidents to the level of complete individual concepts and extrinsic denominations. For even if it is less than clear whether Solomon is a constituent of "father of Solomon," surely the concept <Solomon> is included in the extrinsic denomination <father of Solomon>. So, if we maintain that <father of Solomon> is included in <David>, then, by the transitivity of inclusion, <Solomon> is included in <David>. In fact, this result might seem to lend credibility to the claim that Leibniz would have regarded Solomon as a constituent of "father of Solomon." If <Solomon> is included in <father of Solomon>, then why wouldn't Solomon, the individual, be contained in the accident "father of Solomon"? Surprising though it may seem, however, <Solomon> is not included in <father of Solomon>. And if <Solomon> is not included in <father of Solomon>, then even if <father of Solomon> is included in <David>, the concept <Solomon> need not be, as the antecedent conditions of transitivity are simply not met. Solomon's complete individual concept is only included in itself and does not get a foothold in David's concept. An adequate showing of this requires consideration of Leibniz's views on the formal properties of concept-inclusion and the structure of complex concepts, and it is to this that I now turn.

III. Concepts, Concept-Inclusion and the Non-Inclusion of Individual Concepts in Extrinsic Denominations

As discussed in the preceding chapter, according to Leibniz, concepts come in two varieties: simple and complex. Simple concepts admit of no structural analysis; they are conceived through themselves[7] and have no components. Complex concepts do have structure, as they are formed out of simpler concepts. Most often, Leibniz states that complex concepts are formed out of simpler ones by means of an operation called real addition and also the negation operation.[8] Though I do not believe this was the only method of forming complex concepts that Leibniz recognized, he surely devotes most of his discussions of the topic to this method.[9] For example, the concept <Man> is the real sum of the concepts <Rational> and <Animal>, and, of course, <Rational> and <Animal> are themselves complex concepts formed by real addition. Leibniz says explicitly that the real addition operation is idempotent and commutative,[10] but commentators have pointed out that the proofs Leibniz offers for some of his theorems presuppose that the operation is associative as well.[11]

Leibniz formulates his notion of one concept's inclusion or containment in another in various ways, though he appears to view them all as equivalent. He sometimes says that a concept A is included in a concept B if and only if it is not possible for an object to fall under the concept B but not under A.[12]

So, the concept <rational> is included in the real sum <rational animal> since any object which fell under the concept <rational animal> would also have to fall under <rational>. But even with this formulation of concept-inclusion, we can already see that <Solomon> is not included in <father of Solomon>. Is it possible for an individual to fall under the concept <father of Solomon> without also falling under <Solomon>? I certainly hope so. Even a science fiction author who believes the only thing preventing one from traveling back through time and becoming one's own father is that we do not yet have fast enough rockets would admit that it is at least *possible* for an individual to be the father of Solomon without also being Solomon.

Another more formal definition of concept-inclusion from Leibniz's "Calculus of Real Addition" (among other places) states that a concept A is included in B if and only if there is some concept N (which may be simple or complex), such that the real sum of A and N is B.[13] Using the "+" for real addition and "≤" for concept-inclusion,[14] the foregoing definition may be partially symbolized as follows:

(15) $A \leq B$ iff for some concept N, $A+N=B$.

Thus, <rational> is included in <rational animal>, for there is a concept <animal> which, when combined with <rational> via real addition, yields <rational animal>. From (15) and other theorems, Leibniz derives the following formal test for concept-inclusion, which I believe provides the most instructive explication of his understanding of concept-inclusion of any of his formulations of that notion:

(16) $A \leq B$ iff $A+B=B$.[15]

As will soon be seen, <Solomon> is not included in <the father of Solomon> because it fails the test for inclusion presented in (16).

The application of (16) to test for one concept's inclusion in another will be greatly facilitated if we consider Leibniz's views on the extensions of complex concepts. For Leibniz, the extension of a complex concept A+B is the intersection of the extension of A with the extension of B.[16] In a recent paper by Chris Swoyer, the preceding account of the extension of a complex concept is expressed in the following formal definition:

(17) $\text{ext}(A+B) = \text{ext}(A) \cap \text{ext}(B)$ (where "ext" is a function that assigns a set of individuals as an extension to each concept).[17]

And we may add to this the extremely plausible observation that if two concepts are identical, then so are their extensions.[18] Or, stated contrapositively,

Extrinsic Denominations and Where Accidents Are Allowed to Put Their Feet   41

(18) For any concepts A and B, if ext (A) ≠ ext (B), then A ≠ B.

With (16)-(18) in hand, it can now be shown that <Solomon> is not included in <the father of Solomon>. Let S represent the concept <Solomon> and F the concept <the father of Solomon>. Then, by (17), ext (S+F)= ext (S) ∩ ext (F). Ext (S) is a set whose sole member is Solomon (the individual), and ext (F) is a set whose sole member is David (the individual). The intersection of those two sets is therefore the empty set. From this, we can see that ext (S+F) ≠ ext (F), since ext (S+F), as just shown, is the empty set, and ext (F) is a set whose only member is David. Given this, it follows, by (18), that S+F ≠ F, which, by (16), implies that ~(S ≤ F).

Of course, this result is not peculiar to <the father of Solomon>. The above showing can be generalized. That is, it can be shown that

(19) For any extrinsic denomination, D, of any individual, *I*, and any concept, C, such that C is a component of D[19] and C is a concept of an individual other than *I*, C is not included in D.

Let D be an extrinsic denomination of an individual *I*, and let C be a component of D which is a concept of an individual other than *I*. Then by (17), ext (C+D)= ext (C) ∩ ext (D). The extension of C will often be a set consisting of one member. But there are cases where more than one individual will fall under C. In any case, whatever the extension of C, we know, by the antecedent stipulations in (19), that *I* will not be in C's extension. *I* is an individual other than whatever individuals fall under C. As for the extension of D since, by stipulation, D is an extrinsic denomination of *I*, we know that *I* is in D's extension. Thus, the set formed by ext (C) ∩ ext (D) will not have *I* as an element (that is, *I* ∈ ext (C) and *I* ∉ ext (D), so ext (C) ∩ ext (D) will not contain *I*). This means that ext (C+D) ≠ ext (D), for as just shown, *I* is not an element of ext (C+D), but is an element of ext (D). It follows, then, by (18), that C+D ≠ D. And this, by (16), yields the desired result that ~(C ≤ D).

It has become exceedingly clear, then, that individual concepts are not included in extrinsic denominations. This fact defeats the earlier charge that, because of the transitivity of inclusion, Solomon's complete individual concept is included in both David's concept and Solomon's concept. <Solomon> simply is not included in David's concept, even if <father of Solomon> is. I believe this result further suggests that Leibniz would not regard Solomon, the individual, as a constituent of the relational accident "father of Solomon." It would be surprising to say the least if Leibniz regarded the concept of Solomon as not being included in <father of Solomon>, but still viewed Solomon as being a constituent of "father of Solomon." The result we have reached at the level of concepts thus provides support for a rejection of Cover and Hawthorne's argument at the level of accidents. Now, Cover and Hawthorne complain more than once in their book about the tendency of some of Leibniz's interpreters (Russell and Couturat chief among them) to draw results about Leibniz's metaphysics from his logic.[20] And, of course, my last suggestion would count as an example of this. I do believe that there is generally a very close connection between logic and metaphysics in Leibniz, and that one can frequently gain insight into his views on one by examining his views on the other. In any case, even Cover and Hawthorne would not claim that Leibniz's logic and metaphysics *must* diverge. Thus, the mere claim that some of Leibniz's interpreters move back and forth far too uncritically between Leibniz's logic and metaphysics does not by itself undermine my earlier contention. Indeed, I believe that the non-inclusion of individual concepts in extrinsic denominations, together with the inherent strangeness of the notion that individuals are constituents of relational accidents, imposes upon Cover and Hawthorne the need to explain why, according to Leibniz, individuals are nevertheless constituents of those accidents, not to mention what it means to say that they are.

IV. What the Structure of Extrinsic Denominations Is Not

Extrinsic denominations are concepts that have component concepts; in other words, they are complex concepts. It has also emerged, though, that they are complex concepts some of whose component concepts are not included in them. This fact, as shown previously, provides the basis for a response to a formidable criticism (based on the transitivity of inclusion) against the view that extrinsic denominations are properties that are included in the concepts of the things they denominate and that relational accidents are genuine accidents of individuals. But something is still amiss here. Leibniz appears to have only real addition (and negation) as the means of forming complex concepts out of simpler ones. This would mean that since extrinsic denominations are complex concepts, they are also constructed via real addition. Yet he also says that all the component concepts of a real sum are included in the complex concept constituted by that sum. In Definition 4 from his *Study in the Calculus of Real Addition*, he writes

> 'B + N = L' means that B is in L, or, that L contains B, and that B and N together constitute or compose L. The same holds for a larger number of terms.[21]

So, if an extrinsic denomination is a real sum, then all of its components should be included in it. However, as shown above, other principles and results of Leibniz's logic of concepts imply that some of the component concepts of extrinsic denominations are not included in those denominations. Clearly, something is awry.

Extrinsic Denominations and Where Accidents Are Allowed to Put Their Feet 43

The resolution of this problem lies in recognizing that extrinsic denominations are not expressible as real sums. Extrinsic denominations, though they are assuredly complex concepts and are formed out of simpler concepts in *some* manner, cannot be so formed by combining simpler concepts via real addition. It is highly plausible to maintain that to adequately form the concept of any extrinsic denomination, the concept of the individual(s) other than the one denominated must be a component of it. We cannot, for example, form the concept <the father of Solomon> without employing the concept <Solomon> as a component. Anything which purports to be a formal representation of <the father of Solomon> but which utterly leaves out of the representation a term corresponding to <Solomon> is simply not what it purports to be. So, if the only way we have to represent the structure of <the father of Solomon> is as a real sum all of whose components, by Leibniz's Definition 4 above, are included, and <Solomon> is not included in that sum, then it seems right to conclude that <the father of Solomon> simply is not a real sum. And this is true for any extrinsic denomination. All extrinsic denominations, to be adequately formed or conceived, require as components the concepts of individuals other than the one(s) they denominate, but according to (19), such concepts are never included, and thus extrinsic denominations cannot be real sums, for all the components of real sums are included. Hence, no extrinsic denomination is a real sum.

This can be seen in another way as well. Given the earlier assumption that any adequate representation of an extrinsic denomination must have as a component a concept of the individual(s) other than the one denominated, then if <the father of Solomon> is to be expressed as a real sum, its structure must be of the form $(C_1 + C_2 + \ldots + C_n + <Solomon>)$. That is, <Solomon> must be tacked on by real addition to whatever other concepts are needed to form <the father of Solomon>. But it can be shown that no real sum having <Solomon> as a component can represent the concept <the father of Solomon>. It is intuitively obvious that ext (<the father of Solomon>) = {David}. But ext $(C_1 + C_2 + \ldots + C_n + <Solomon>)$ = ext $(C_1) \cap$ ext $(C_2) \cap \ldots$ ext $(C_n) \cap$ ext (<Solomon>). Now, ext (<Solomon>) = {Solomon}. Therefore either ext $(C_1 + C_2 + \ldots + C_n + <Solomon>)$ = {Solomon} (if Solomon is in the extension of any of the other concepts), or it will equal the empty set (if Solomon is not in the extension of any of the other concepts). In either case, ext (<the father of Solomon>) ≠ ext $(C_1 + C_2 \ldots + C_n + <Solomon>)$, and so, by (18), $(C_1 + C_2 + \ldots + C_n + <Solomon>)$ ≠ <the father of Solomon>. And this means that <the father of Solomon> is not expressible as any real sum in which one of the components in the sum is <Solomon>. Yet since <Solomon> must be involved in any adequate representation of <the father of Solomon>, <the father of Solomon> is not a real sum. The same could be shown for any extrinsic denomination.

It also bears pointing out that extrinsic denominations are not the only type of complex concept that is not expressible as a real sum. Certain intrinsic denominations also cannot be expressed as real sums. Take the intrinsic denomination <a blue-eyed man>. It seems we cannot help but assume that <blue> is a component concept of this denomination; the denomination must involve <blue> in some way. It can be shown, however, that <blue> is not included in the denomination. From (16), we know that if <blue> is included in <a blue-eyed man>, then <blue> + <a blue-eyed man> = <a blue-eyed man>. But ext (<blue> + <a blue-eyed man>) = ext (<blue>) ∩ ext (<a blue-eyed man>). Now, ext (<blue>) = the set of all blue things and ext (<a blue-eyed man>) = the set of all blue-eyed men. The intersection of the two will then be the set of all blue things which are blue-eyed men, and clearly this does not equal the set of all blue-eyed men (there are at least some blue-eyed men who are not blue!). So, ext (<blue> + <a blue-eyed man>) ≠ ext (<a blue-eyed man>), which means (<blue> + <a blue-eyed man>) ≠ <a blue-eyed man>, which, in turn, means <blue> is not included in <a blue-eyed man>. The upshot of this is that no real sum which has <blue> as a component can express the concept <a blue-eyed man>, since by Definition 4, all the components of real sums are included and since <blue> is not included in <a blue-eyed man>. And because <blue> seemingly must be part of the concept <a blue-eyed man>, then <a blue-eyed man> is not expressible as a real sum. The same could be shown for other intrinsic denominations, such as <a brown-haired woman>, <a long-armed person>, etc.[22]

It is clear, then, that real addition is not nearly rich enough to render the structure of all our concepts. And it should be pointed out that this inadequacy of real addition will exist regardless of whether extrinsic denominations are properties or not. Nevertheless, the important point for present purposes is that extrinsic denominations are not real sums. For this provides the means of resolving the earlier problem of how it could be that extrinsic denominations are real sums and yet still have non-included component concepts.

There are some fairly clear indications that Leibniz was aware that some of the component concepts required to conceive something may not be included in the concept of that thing. In a significant passage from his correspondence with DeVolder, Leibniz writes

> Who will deny, too, that one substance is modified by the intervention of another, as when a body is repelled by some obstacle in its path? In order to conceive the rebound of one of these bodies, therefore, the concept of both of them will be necessary, yet the rebound can be the modification of only one, since the other may continue in its path without rebound. Something more is needed in the definition of a modification, therefore, than the necessity of another con-

cept, and to be 'contained in' [i.e., included in] . . . is more than to need something else. In my opinion there is nothing in the whole created universe which does not need, for its perfect concept, the concept of everything else in the universality of things, since everything flows into every other thing in such a way that if anything is removed or changed, everything in the world will be different from what it now is.[23]

Leibniz appears here to state explicitly that not every concept *needed* to conceive something is included in the concept of that thing. We need the concept <Solomon> to conceive of <the father of Solomon>, but <Solomon> is not included in <the father of Solomon>.

Further, in an essay entitled *General Inquiries about the Analysis of Concepts and of Truths*,[24] Leibniz appears to countenance another way of forming complex concepts out of simpler ones besides real addition. In the essay, he distinguishes between what he calls "direct" addition and "oblique" addition. It is clear from Leibniz's discussion that direct addition is the same operation as real addition. Oblique addition, however, is the forming of complex concepts out of simpler ones through "the mediation of particles or syncategorematic terms [e.g., 'in' and 'of']."[25] As an example, Leibniz says that <of Evander> can be obliquely added to <sword> to form <the sword of Evander>.[26] And as <the sword of Evander> is clearly an extrinsic denomination, Leibniz's discussion here perhaps shows that he realized that extrinsic denominations were not expressible as real sums. Unfortunately, though Leibniz makes impressive efforts to develop the formal contours of real (or direct) addition and the concept-inclusion relation, both in this essay and others, he has little else to say about oblique addition. We must therefore remain relatively in the dark about how Leibniz would have rendered the formal structure of oblique sums. Despite this uncertainty, I believe we can say that Leibniz realized there was more to forming complex concepts than merely conjoining simpler ones by real addition.

Chapter Four

Extrinsic Denominations and the Interconnection of All Things

I. Introduction

In this chapter, I examine another argument Leibniz frequently puts forth to establish NPE. In this argument, Leibniz argues that because all things are interconnected (hereafter referred to as IC), there are no purely extrinsic denominations. Perhaps the most well-known passage containing the IC argument occurs in the *New Essays*:

> *Philalethes*. However, a change of relation can occur without there having been any change in the subject: Titius, 'whom I consider today as a father, ceases to be so tomorrow, only by the death of his son, without any alteration made in himself.'
> *Theophilus*. That can very well be said if we are guided by the things of which we are aware; but in metaphysical strictness there is no wholly extrinsic denomination, because of the real connections amongst all things.[1]

As was true of the PS argument, the argument here appears rather simple. The only premise Leibniz, through the person of Theophilus, offers for NPE is IC. Yet despite the simplicity of its structure, the argument is not at all easy to reconstruct. First, IC, its premise, must be interpreted, and this task is not as easy as one might hope, for Leibniz never explicitly defines IC. However, Leibniz's pronouncements on the doctrine do permit the reaching of a relatively high level of certainty as to what he meant by it, and an examination of these pronouncements will be the subject of section II of this chapter. The result of the examination is that when Leibniz asserts IC he is claiming that a change in one thing entails a change in every other. Second, it is not easy to see why Leibniz would even want to infer NPE in the context of the IC argument. As the quote from the *New Essays* indicates, Leibniz is concerned with the issue of whether a thing changes whenever one of its extrinsic denominations does. The passage also shows that Leibniz believes that things do change whenever their extrinsic denominations do, and this is just what (9) from chapter two maintains. In the PS argument for NPE, Leibniz derives NPE from PS and then obtains (9) from NPE. As I will explain in section III, (9) is virtually an immediate consequence of IC, and so since (9) is the conclusion Leibniz seems to want in the IC argument, the question arises of why Leibniz concludes NPE rather than (9) in the argument. In section IV, I argue that the answer to this question lies in understanding the underlying context of the IC argument. In the passage from the *New Essays,* Philalethes represents Locke, and Philalethes's view is the one set forth in the corresponding passage of Locke's *Essay.* Locke's (Philalethes's) claim that changes of extrinsic denomination can occur without a change in the denominated thing is, I show in section IV, a consequence of his belief that extrinsic denominations are not properties. This inferential relationship between the two claims provides the answer to why Leibniz infers NPE rather than (9), for NPE can be viewed as a response to the claim that extrinsic denominations are not properties.

With IC interpreted and the Lockean context of the argument explained, I then turn to the task of reconstructing the argument. In section V, I set forth a reconstruction of the argument with its conclusion read as (6), which asserts that there are no extrinsic denominations of a thing that are not included in the concept of that thing. This assertion is nothing less than the claim that extrinsic denominations *are* properties of what they denominate and is thus an exceedingly appropriate thing for Leibniz to conclude in the IC argument. I also show that (6) follows directly from IC under the construal of the Lockean context I offer in section IV. After discussing an objection to my interpretation in section VI, I suggest, in section VII, various reductionist reconstructions of the argument. They all suffer from two significant defects: the reductionist version of NPE makes no sense as something Leibniz would assert as a response to Locke, and it simply does not follow from IC. In section VIII, I consider another interpretation of NPE, different from both my reading and the reductionists', that is not beset with the difficulties of the reductionist view but, like the reductionist view, asserts a correlation between extrinsic and intrinsic denominations. I argue that, though this alternative view avoids the problems the reductionist view faces in this setting, it does not fit well in other contexts in which Leibniz asserts NPE and is thus not a plausible reading of NPE overall. I devote section IX of the chapter to showing how my reading of NPE would follow from IC under an alternative construal of the Lockean context. Although I believe Locke reasons from the claim that extrinsic denominations are not properties to the claim that extrinsic denominations can change without a change occurring in the denominated thing, some of Locke's interpreters see Locke's inference as running in the opposite direction. I argue that my reading of NPE still fits quite well as the conclusion of the IC argument even against this backdrop. The conclusion that emerges

Extrinsic Denominations and the Interconnection of All Things 49

from the chapter is that, as was the case with regard to the PS argument, my reading of NPE forms an excellent fit with the argument, while the reductionist reading does not fit well at all, and is therefore unlikely to have been what Leibniz had in mind.

II. On the Meaning of Interconnection

The first step to reconstructing the argument is to gain a clear understanding of IC. As mentioned, Leibniz never favors us with an explicit definition of the doctrine. Surprisingly few interpreters have discussed the doctrine at any length, and much that has been written has been less than satisfying.[2] Nevertheless, as will be shown, Leibniz does say enough about IC to enable one to arrive at a reasonably clear understanding of what he meant by it. In chapter two,[3] I claimed that IC should be understood as

(12) A change in one thing entails a change in every other.

I believe the following textual considerations show that (12) renders IC correctly. Leibniz's basic reason for believing IC was that the physical universe is a plenum. In the *Principles of Nature and Grace*, he says," because the world is a plenum everything is connected together, and each body acts on every other body more or less according to the distance, and is affected by it by reaction."[4] A plenum is such that a movement in any of its members results in, and indeed cannot occur without, a movement in every other member as well.[5] Now, for Leibniz, the concepts of motion and change are closely related to one another. First, motion is itself a type of change.[6] Second, all other types of change can be explained in terms of motion.[7] Thus, if a thing is moving, it is changing; and if a thing is changing, it is moving. Thus, since in a plenum if one member moves, all of the members move, and since all change involves motion, then if one thing changes, there will be a movement and, consequently, a change in every other.

Elsewhere, when Leibniz explains how IC arises from the fact that the universe is a plenum, he describes IC as being the same as Hippocrates's claim that, "all things conspire."[8] In *A Specimen of Discoveries about Marvelous Secrets*, he provides this clear statement of the meaning of the Hippocratic claim, a statement which for all intents and purposes is (12):

> [W]hat Hippocrates said about the human body is true of the whole universe: namely, that all things conspire and are sympathetic, i.e., that nothing happens in one creature of which some exactly corresponding effect does not reach all others.[9]

It should be noted that though Leibniz infers IC from the fact that the realm of bodies is a plenum, IC applies to monads as well as bodies. For a monad *expresses*[10] the particular body with which it is involved, and since that body is connected with every other in the plenum, then every change that occurs in that body as a result of a change in another will be reflected in the monad's expression of that body. As Leibniz explains to Arnauld,

> Because of the continuity and divisibility of all matter, the slightest movement exerts its effect upon near-by bodies, and so from body to body to infinity, but in diminishing proportion. So our body must be affected in some way by the changes of all the rest. Now to all the motions of our body there correspond certain perceptions or thoughts of our soul, more or less confused; thus the soul will have some thought of all the motions of the universe, and in my opinion every other soul or substance will have some perception or expression of it.[11]

It is quite appropriate, then, to say that IC applies to monads as well as bodies.

Finally, consider the following argument for NPE, which is clearly another instance of the IC argument:

> A relation seems difficult to distinguish from other predicates, for any action requires something that is acted upon, magnitude consists in comparison, quality in a disposition to action. Therefore, extrinsic denominations, which arise and disappear without any change in the subject itself but only because a change comes about in something else, appear to pertain properly to Relation; thus a father becomes a father when the child is born, even if he happens to be in India and thus is not affected. Thus my similitude to someone else arises without any change in me, solely by change in the other person. It must be admitted, however, that speaking rigorously there is no extrinsic denomination in reality, since nothing happens anywhere in the universe which does not affect every existent thing in the universe.[12]

In this passage, Leibniz again discusses cases in which it seems that a change of extrinsic denomination occurs without a change in the denominated thing, but solely by a change in something other than the denominated thing. Here, as in the earlier passage from the *New Essays,* he says that though such cases appear to occur, in reality there are no purely extrinsic denominations. Yet in the second passage, instead of offering the interconnection of all things as the premise for NPE, he appeals to what is essentially (12). The similarity of the two passages, together with the considerations presented in the preceding two paragraphs, demonstrate that the premise offered for NPE in the second passage—(12)—is simply a more elaborated version of the premise offered in the first, namely IC. Thus, in reconstructing the IC argument for NPE, I shall henceforth treat (12) as its central premise.

III. A Puzzle Concerning the IC Argument

In both of the above-quoted instances of the IC argument for NPE, Leibniz considers cases in which it appears that a thing's extrinsic denominations change as a result of a change in some other thing and without any change in the thing denominated. Now, a change in a thing's extrinsic denominations can result from one of two occurrences. A change of extrinsic denominations can occur as a result of a change in the denominated thing or it can occur solely as a result of a change in something other than the denominated thing. For ease of discussion, let us refer to changes in the former category as Type A changes and those in the latter category as type B changes. Suppose Jones and some object Q initially have no properties in common, but then Jones takes on some property F, which Q also has. Because of this, the extrinsic denomination <similar to Q> has now become true of Jones. This sort of a change in Jones's extrinsic denominations would be an instance of a Type A change. But a change in Q's extrinsic denominations has occurred as well. The extrinsic denomination <similar to Jones> has now become true of Q, and that change has occurred solely as a result of a change in Jones, not Q, thus making it a Type B change. Clearly, type A changes of extrinsic denomination are always accompanied by a change in the denominated thing. But does the denominated thing also change in type B cases? As the earlier quoted instances of the IC argument for NPE show, Leibniz would answer that question in the affirmative.

Indeed, it is a straightforward consequence of IC, when construed in the manner of (12), that the denominated individual changes in type B cases. (12) says that a change in one thing entails a change in every other. In type B cases, a thing's extrinsic denominations change as a result of a change in another thing. And so it follows by IC that in type B cases the denominated thing changes as well. With this in mind, we can see that IC provides another way of establishing proposition (9) from chapter two. Namely,

> (9) As often as the (extrinsic) denomination of a thing is changed, there must be some variation in the thing itself.

As we saw in chapter two, Leibniz derives NPE from PS and then uses NPE to prove (9). (9), however, can be directly inferred from IC, without the prior establishment of NPE.

That (9) follows directly from IC raises a puzzle concerning the IC argument for NPE. If the point of the IC argument is merely to show that the denominated thing changes in type B cases, then (9) would have been just the right thing for Leibniz to conclude in the argument. He could have listed his examples of cases in which it seems that a change of extrinsic denomination occurs without a change in the denominated individual, and then, in place of NPE, asserted that, in metaphysical strictness, there are no such cases—i.e., (9)—because of the interconnection of all things. Why, then, is NPE the conclusion of the IC argument rather than (9)?

If one had only the IC argument to go by, then given the way Leibniz presents the argument, one might be tempted to say that (9) *just is* what Leibniz meant by NPE. In fact, Massimo Mugnai appears to adopt this view of NPE for this very reason.[13] But though (9) and NPE are closely connected in the thought of Leibniz, I believe it would be a serious mistake to regard them as one and the same claim. As was seen in the PS argument from *Primary Truths*, Leibniz appears to distinguish the two claims from one another: he first derives NPE from PS and then derives (9) from NPE. Moreover, it is difficult to see how (9) could be the conclusion of the PS argument. For in order for (9) to serve in that capacity, it has to make sense for Leibniz to assert, "there are no extrinsic denominations of a thing that can change without a change occurring in that thing, which have no foundation in the thing." That is, it has to make sense to regard an extrinsic denomination that *can* change without a change occurring in the denominated thing as an extrinsic denomination that has no foundation in the thing denominated, where a foundation, as shown in chapter two, is understood as that which provides a reason and an *a priori* proof for the proposition having that extrinsic denomination as its predicate. That the denominated thing changes whenever its extrinsic denominations change does not guarantee that propositions having that thing's concept as subject and an extrinsic denomination of that thing as predicate will be identical. Consider again the earlier example of Jones and Q. As a result of a change in Jones, Q takes on the extrinsic denomination <similar to Jones>. And suppose, in accord with the view that reads NPE as (9), we maintain that this change in Q's extrinsic denominations is accompanied by a change in Q. Will this guarantee that the proposition "Q is similar to Jones" is identical? Not unless what has changed in Q is that it now has the extrinsic denomination <similar to Jones>, which it formerly lacked. And (9), by itself, just does not guarantee that. (9) asserts only that *something* changes in the denominated thing whenever one of its extrinsic denominations changes. When Q takes on <similar to Jones> it could be that the change occuring in Q is that one of its hairs becomes white. That the change in Q's extrinsic denomination is accompanied by *that* change certainly does not provide any assurance that "Q is similar to Jones" is an identical proposition (in Leibniz's sense). (9) just does not line up with the PS principle and that principle's connections to the foundations, reasons, and a priori proofs of truth. It is thus not a good candidate for an interpretation of NPE. (I present Mugnai's view in more detail and offer additional criticisms of it in the Appendix.)

It would also be problematic to claim that Leibniz accepted alternative (and presumably) equivalent formulations of NPE, such that in the PS argument, for example, he has one formulation in mind, but that in the IC argument he has (9) in mind, and so on. Leibniz does propose alternative formulations for some of his important ideas, such as the notion of concept inclusion. In some passages, he says that a concept A is included in a concept B if and only if it is impossible for an object to fall under B but not under A.[14] In other places, he states that A is included in B if and only if the real sum of A and B is just B.[15] And he appears to regard the diverse formulations as equivalent. But it would be little more than sheer conjecture to suppose that Leibniz accepted multiple formulations of NPE. Leibniz never explicitly defines NPE, and so never explicitly provides alternative formulations of NPE. The only evidence that he accepted alternative formulations of NPE would be that one formulation, on the surface, seems to fit better in some passages, while another formulation seems to work better in others. Such a view is possible, but, absent any explicit contrary indications from Leibniz, it is surely preferable to seek a single understanding of NPE that works well in all of the relevant passages.

IV. The Lockean Context

An essential step to reaching a satisfying solution to the puzzle is to understand the broader context in which Leibniz offers the IC argument. The earlier quoted version of the IC argument from Leibniz's *New Essays* is, as discussed in the introduction to this chapter, a rebuttal to a passage from Locke's *Essay*. In Book II, ch. XXV, sec. 5, Locke asserts that

(20) A thing's extrinsic denominations (or "external denominations," as he terms them) can change without any change occurring in that thing.

In section 8 of the same chapter, Locke also claims that relations and extrinsic denominations are not ideas "contained in the real existence of things, but something extraneous and superinduced." At a minimum, this states that

(21) Extrinsic denominations are not *in* (or are not properties of) what they denominate.

An examination of (20) and (21) suggests that one who accepted both may very well also believe that the two claims stand in an inferential relation to one another. Whether a denomination is or is not a property of the denominated thing is quite relevant to the question of whether the denominated thing changes upon gaining or losing that denomination, and vice versa. And I believe that Locke viewed the two as inferentially related. Further, I believe that understanding the precise way in which he viewed them as related is the key to solving the puzzle of why Leibniz infers NPE rather than (9) in the IC argument.

Some of Locke's interpreters have conjectured that (20) was his reason, or at least one of his reasons, for claiming (21). The following quote form Woolhouse is exemplary:

> Relations are extraneous and superinduced because some relative terms can cease to apply to an object without there being any change in that thing. Caius ceases to be a father when his *son dies* (II.xxv.5). One door ceases to be the same colour as another when the *other* door is *painted*.[16]

Certainly, if a denomination can be gained or lost without any change in the denominated thing, then that is good reason to believe that such a denomination is not in, or is not a property of, the denominated thing. However, this interpretation of Locke suffers from a conspicuous absence of textual support. In no passage does Locke claim or even imply that (20) is his justification for (21). In the only passage in which Locke could be viewed as connecting (20) and (21), which is in chapter 25, section 5, Locke's reasoning, as will be discussed below, is most naturally understood as moving from (21) to (20), not the other way around. In saying this, I do not mean to assert that Locke would not think (20), assuming independent grounds could be given for it, provides good reason for accepting (21). I am merely claiming that there are no grounds for believing he offers (20) as support for (21) in the *Essay*.[17]

A closer examination of Locke's treatment of relations and extrinsic denominations reveals that Locke ultimately intends (21) to be grounds for accepting (20), instead of (20) as grounds for (21). To see this, we must first gain a better understanding of how Locke conceives of relations and extrinsic denominations. Well before he presents (20), Locke begins his chapter on relations with these words:

> Besides the ideas, whether simple of complex, that the mind has of things, as they are in themselves, there are others it gets from their comparison one with another. The understanding, in the consideration of any thing, is not confined to that precise object: it can carry any idea, as it were, beyond itself, or, at least, look beyond it, to see how it stands in conformity to any other. When the mind so considers one thing, that it does, as it were, bring it to, and set by another, and carry its view from one to t'other: this is as the words import, *relation* and *respect*; and the denominations given to positive things, intimating that respect and serving as marks to lead the thoughts beyond the subject itself denominated, to something distinct from it, are what we call *relatives*.[18]

Locke's term "relatives" appears to designate what Leibniz labels "extrinsic denominations." As the quote indicates, our ideas of relations and extrinsic denominations are not ideas of things as they are in themselves. We acquire our ideas of them by comparing things in some respect or other. To take one of Locke's examples, we can ascribe the extrinsic denomination <whiter> to Caius by virtue of comparing the white color of Caius to the white color of free-stone.[19] For Locke, <whiter> is not a property of Caius. The only property Caius has in this regard is the intrinsic denomination <white>, and his being denominated <whiter> is merely the result of comparing him with free-stone in respect of each one's white color. Locke reiterates this point in section 2:

> But all names, that are more than empty sounds, must signify some idea, which is either in the thing to which the name is applied; and then it is positive, and is looked on as united to, and existing in the thing to which the denomination is given: or else it arises from the respect the mind finds in it, to something distinct from it, with which it considers it; and then it includes a relation.[20]

This passage clearly implies that names that include relations (that is, relatives or extrinsic denominations) do not correspond to any idea that is in the denominated thing; rather, they correspond to ideas that the mind acquires by comparing two things with each other in some respect.

With this bit of background on how Locke understands relations and extrinsic denominations, we are now in a position to see that Locke does indeed offer (21) in support of (20), and not the other way around. In section 5 when Locke presents (20), he does so in the following way:

> The nature therefore of relation, consists in the referring, or comparing two things, one to another; from which comparison, one or both comes to be denominated. And if either of those things be removed, or cease to be, the relation ceases, and the denomination consequent to it, though the other receive in itself no alteration at all. E.g. Caius, whom I consider to day as a father, ceases to be so to morrow, only by the death of his son, without any alteration made in himself.[21]

The first sentence of the quote restates the understanding of relations and extrinsic denominations Locke sets forth in sections 1 and 2, and as described in the preceding paragraph. A relation just is a comparison between two things, and extrinsic denominations are the denominations that result from relations. They are not properties of the related or denominated things. The second sentence is Locke's assertion of (20).[22] The second sentence begins with the word "and," and this fact makes it rather unlikely that the second sentence is being put forth as support for the first. It would have been awkward for Locke to assert in the first sentence that relations and extrinsic denominations are just the results of the mind's comparing one thing to another, and then say,

"*And* a change of extrinsic denomination can occur without a change in the denominated thing," in the next, if he meant to put forth the second sentence as support for the first. However, that the second sentence begins with "And" does allow for the first sentence to be reason for the second, and this is precisely what I believe occurs in the passage. The first sentence presents Locke's general understanding of relations and extrinsic denominations, and the second sentence draws out a consequence of that understanding. To see this, consider Locke's example of Caius. Caius, when compared to his son in the relevant respect (whatever that may be, for Locke) stands in a paternity relation to his son, and as a result, Caius bears the extrinsic denomination <father>. As a consequence of a change in his son (viz., his son's death), Caius loses the denomination <father>. In Locke's language, because Caius's son has ceased to be, the relation between him and Caius has also ceased along with the denomination consequent to it. Yet although Caius undergoes this change as a result of a change in his son, that fact by itself does not show that no change has occurred in Caius. For the change of extrinsic denomination could itself constitute a change in Caius. It could, that is, if extrinsic denominations were properties. But on Locke's conception of relations and extrinsic denominations, as invoked in the first sentence of the passage, extrinsic denominations are not properties. Consequently, since the change in Caius's extrinsic denomination comes about only through a change in his son and since the change of extrinsic denomination is not itself constitutive of a change in Caius, as extrinsic denominations are not properties, then Caius can lose the denomination without any change occurring in him.[23] This, I maintain, is Locke's argument in section 5.[24] And, more importantly for present purposes, it is to this argument that Leibniz responds with the IC argument for NPE.

V. The IC Argument with NPE Interpreted as (6)

Given this interpretation of Locke's argument in section 5, we are now in a position to understand why Leibniz counters with NPE rather than (9) in the corresponding section of the *New Essays*—we are, that is, if NPE is interpreted as (6). In section IV, as we have seen, Locke invokes (21) as grounds for inferring (20). In other words, Locke claims that if (21) is true, then (20) is true. Leibniz's response to this in section 5 of the *New Essays* is that there are no purely extrinsic denominations because of the interconnection of all things. As was shown in section III above, the interconnection of all things, when interpreted as (12), immediately implies that as often as a thing's extrinsic denominations change there will be a change in that thing, which is proposition (9). Now, (9) represents the negation of (20), and if (20) is false, then—since Locke accepts that if (21) is true, then (20) is true—(21) is false as well. That is, it is false that extrinsic denominations are not properties of what they denominate. It is not the case that extrinsic denominations are not in what they denominate, and this is just what NPE when interpreted as (6) maintains. Leibniz was not merely objecting to (20); if that were all he had had in mind, he could have simply offered (9) on the grounds of IC, which would cause his actual inference to NPE to appear odd and inappropriate. However, Locke argues that because extrinsic denominations are not in what they denominate—i.e., (21)—they can change without any change occurring in the denominated thing—i.e., (20). It is thus entirely fitting for Leibniz to counter this by arguing that, because a change in one thing entails a change in every other (i.e., IC) then whenever a thing's extrinsic denominations change, as a result of a change in something else, there is a change in that thing (which is (9) and which negates (20)), and therefore extrinsic denominations *are* in what they denominate—i.e., NPE interpreted is (6).

The preceding reconstruction of the IC argument for NPE assumes, of course, that Leibniz also interpreted Locke as putting forth (21) as grounds for (20) in the *Essay*. I believe that, independently of the issue of whether Leibniz interprets Locke this way, regarding Locke as inferring (20) from (21) is the best representation that can be given of Locke's reasoning in his section 5. Now Leibniz never explicitly states that he views Locke's argument in this way. But as it does appear to be the correct rendering of Locke's argument, I believe that, absent any contrary indications from Leibniz, we can justifiably presume that Leibniz did read Locke in this manner. I see no such contrary indications in the corresponding sections of Leibniz's *New Essays*. In fact, the structure of Leibniz's presentation in these corresponding sections makes very good sense if we assume that he understood Locke in this manner. In section 1 of Leibniz's Book II, Ch. 25, Philalethes, who represents Locke, restates Locke's basic understanding of relations and extrinsic denominations:

> When the mind compares one thing with another this is 'relation and respect', and the relative terms or denominations which are made from it serve as marks to lead the thoughts beyond the subject ... to something distinct from it.[25]

Theophilus, who represents Leibniz, demonstrates his understanding that this view of the nature of relations carries with it the idea that relations are not real properties of things when he replies, "Relations and orderings are to some extent 'beings of reason', although they have their foundations in things."[26] Significantly, though Philalethes mentions both relations and the (extrinsic) denominations made from them, Theophilus only states that relations and orderings are beings of reason. The status of extrinsic denominations is left open. Leibniz then foregoes commenting on sections 2 through 4 of Locke's chapter 25 and goes directly to section 5 and the IC argument for NPE. After offering his understanding of relations and extrinsic denominations—an understanding that Leibniz construes as including the claim that relations are beings of reason—Philalethes's next statement, then, is the claim that "a change of relation can occur without there having been any change in the subject." That Leibniz arranges his discussion in this manner comports well with the view that he regarded Philalethes's claim in section 1 concerning the ideality of relations and extrinsic denominations as underwriting his claim in section 5 that a change of relation can occur without a change in the subject. For Philalethes, because relations and extrinsic denominations are not in things, but are mere mental constructs, they can change without a change in their subjects. Given this, Theophilus can well respond that, in reality, extrinsic denominations *are* in what they denominate—i.e., NPE construed as (6)—because as often as they change, a change occurs in the denominated thing. Though the sequence of Leibniz's discussion obviously does not constitute conclusive evidence that Leibniz regarded (21) as Locke's grounds for (20), the sequence does at least cohere rather nicely with that view.

VI. A Problem

I have argued that Locke sets forth (21) as grounds for (20). But if this is true, then Locke would also surely accept

(22) If relations (simpliciter) are not properties of the things related, then relations can change without a change occurring in one of the related things.

Locke ascribes the same ontological status to relations as he does to extrinsic denominations. They are both mental constructs. Thus, as Locke says in his section 5, "if either of those [related] things . . . cease to be, the relation ceases, and the denomination consequent to it, though the other receive in itself no alteration at all." Now, (9)—Leibniz's claim that a change of extrinsic denomination is always accompanied by a change in the denominated thing—can easily be extended to prove

(23) A change of relation (simpliciter) is always accompanied by a change in all of the things related.

To see why (23) is true if (9) is true, consider a relation R that holds between a and b. It seems clear, and both Locke and Leibniz would agree, that, as a result of R's holding between a and b (in that order), the extrinsic denomination <an R of b> (or something of roughly that form) is true of a; and, similarly, the extrinsic denomination <*R*'d by *a*>, or the like, is true of *b*. If the relation *R* ceases to hold between *a* and *b*, then the corresponding extrinsic denominations will no longer be true of them either. That is, there will be a change in their extrinsic denominations. And, given (9), we can infer that a change occurs in *a* and *b* as well. Thus, the change in *R* is accompanied by a change in both of the things related by *R*. And, as this would appear to hold for any relation, it follows that (23) is true. The problem is that (22) and (23) together lead to the result that relations *are* properties of the things related, which is a result that Leibniz would surely have rejected. Can Leibniz avoid this result if his reasoning in the IC argument for NPE is as I have interpreted it? I claim Locke argues from (21) to (20). Under my reading of Leibniz's IC argument for NPE, Leibniz also accepts that if (21) is true, then so is (20), but since, by the interconnection of all things, (20) is false, then so is (21). And my reading of NPE is essentially the negation of (21). But now we have seen that Locke also accepts (22), and since Leibniz accepts (9), he is also committed to (23). And it follows from (22) and (23) that relations are properties.

The only way for Leibniz to accept the result for extrinsic denominations while rejecting the analogous result for relations is for him to reject (22). And I believe Leibniz does possess grounds for such a rejection. In other words, Leibniz can believe that relations are not properties, while still believing that all changes of relation are accompanied by a change in each of the related things. Leibniz's acceptance of the doctrine of individual accidents furnishes grounds for accepting the former claim. And (23), which follows from (9), provides grounds for the latter claim. Thus, Leibniz can accept the antecedent of (22) and still deny its consequent. And since (22) is false for Leibniz, he is not saddled with the result that relations are properties.

VII. Possible Reductionist Reconstructions of the IC Argument for NPE

I believe that, quite independently of the insight it offers into Leibniz's IC argument for NPE, regarding Locke as inferring (20) from (21) is the most plausible way to read Locke's section 5. As I have attempted to show, though, it so happens that this reading of Locke also allows one to understand why Leibniz concludes with NPE rather than (9) in the IC argument. Locke believes that if (21) is true, then so is (20). Leibniz, I claim, also believes this, but because his IC doctrine leads immediately to (9), which is the denial of (20); it follows, for Leibniz, that (21) is false as well. And the denial of (21) amounts to NPE—if NPE is read as (6). How, then, is the reductionist to resist this result and provide a reconstruction of the IC argument that leads to the reductionist reading of NPE? There is no question that IC immediately implies (9) or that Leibniz accepted (9). There would thus appear to be two avenues of approach open to the reductionists. They could claim that, though Locke believed (21) implied (20), Leibniz did not, and so, even if (9) shows (20) false, that would not prove (21) false. Under this view, Leibniz's IC argument for NPE would be an attempt to prove invalid Locke's inference of (20) from (21), or to show the conditional, "if (21), then (20)," to be false. The other alternative for reductionists is to reject my reading of the Lockean context, and maintain instead that Locke is actually reasoning from (20) to (21).[27] They would then need a reconstruction of the IC argument in accord with that context and which leads to their version of NPE. For each of the two approaches, I will suggest a reconstruction of the IC argument that I believe reductionists would be likely to offer. And I will argue that neither approach to reconstructing the argument results in a plausible rendering of Leibniz's reasoning.

Suppose that reductionists accept my construction of Locke's section 5 reasoning as the backdrop for understanding Leibniz's IC argument in his section 5. They argue that Locke is reasoning from (21) to (20), but they also believe that, in the IC argument, Leibniz is attempting to show that (21) does not imply (20). Under this approach, Leibniz would, according to reductionists, agree with Locke that extrinsic denominations are not properties of what they denominate—i.e., Leibniz would also accept (21). However, Leibniz disagrees with Locke's claim that this implies that extrinsic denominations can change without a change occurring in the denominated thing. For whenever one thing changes, everything changes (i.e., IC). Now, this all sounds minimally reasonable so far, but what we still lack is an explanation of why Leibniz infers the reductionist version of NPE rather than (9). In other words, we still need an account of why it makes sense for Leibniz to say, roughly, "You may think a thing's extrinsic denominations can change without a change occurring in that thing, but, speaking rigorously, there are no extrinsic denominations that do not reduce to intrinsic ones." Further, we need a showing of how the reductionist version of NPE follows from IC. As I will argue, a reductionist reading of NPE cannot satisfy either of these demands.

Why might Leibniz assert the reducibility of extrinsic denominations to intrinsic ones in this setting? Well, we are assuming that he did not regard extrinsic denominations as properties here. And it may seem that if extrinsic denominations are not properties, things can gain or lose them without undergoing a change, which is how I believe Locke reasons in section 5. It may seem to make sense for Leibniz then to respond that even though extrinsic denominations are not properties, they reduce to intrinsic denominations, which *are* properties, and so when an extrinsic denomination changes, the intrinsic denominations to which they reduce change as well. The reductionist reading of NPE would thus serve as something of a counterexample to Locke's inference to (20) from (21). It is a case in which, though, extrinsic denominations are not properties, the denominated thing still changes as often as its extrinsic denominations do. So, it makes sense for Leibniz to respond to Locke's claim that extrinsic denominations can change without the denominated thing changing with the reductionist version of NPE. There is a glaring difficulty with this account, however. Once we recall the precise sense in which, for reductionists, extrinsic denominations reduce to intrinsic ones, we see that putting forth the claim that extrinsic denominations reduce to intrinsic ones provides no assurance whatsoever that the denominated thing changes.

As discussed in chapter one, the sense in which extrinsic denominations are said to reduce to intrinsic ones is that whatever extrinsic denominations are true of an individual can be inferred from certain intrinsic denominations of that individual and certain intrinsic denominations of the individual(s), to which the given extrinsic denomination relates that individual. To take one of the favored examples of reductionists, consider the extrinsic denomination <similar to B>. That this is true of A can be inferred from the fact that there is some intrinsic denomination, P, which both A and B have. That is, "A is similar to B" follows from the conjunction of "A is now P" and "B is now P." Now, in the IC argument for NPE, Leibniz is primarily concerned with what were earlier labeled type B cases of change—cases where one's extrinsic denominations change because of a change in someone else.[28] Yet these are precisely the cases where reductionist NPE does not guarantee that a change occurs in the denominated thing. Suppose A and B initially have no intrinsic denominations in common. Then B takes on P, which is also an intrinsic denomination of A. The extrinsic denomination <similar to B> then becomes true of A. But what has changed in A? He has had P all along (and still has it), and so it is not that he has P that has changed. The reductionist version only tells us that <similar to B> follows from both A and B's having P; it does not at all imply that A changes when he acquires <similar to B>. Therefore, the reductionist version of NPE simply does not work as a counterexample to Locke's argument from (21) to (20). Someone might respond that perhaps at just the moment when <similar to B> becomes true of A, some intrinsic denomination of A's other than P changes. Such an occurrence is certainly possible, but I am unable to see how it would help here. It must be one of the intrinsic denominations to which the extrinsic denomination reduces that changes. Otherwise, what reason would Leibniz have to assert reductionist NPE in response to Locke? Leibniz should have just said that whenever one of a thing's extrinsic denominations changes, one of its intrinsic denominations changes too. The reductionist reading of NPE just seems to be the wrong thing for Leibniz to say here. Given that Leibniz is primarily concerned to show that type B cases of change are accompanied by a change in the denominated individual, and given also that those are precisely the cases where reductionist NPE offers no assurance that the denominated individual changes, it is implausible in the extreme that reductionist NPE is the conclusion Leibniz has in mind in the IC argument.

If NPE were interpreted as (6), however, it would be just the right sort of thing for Leibniz to assert against Locke. When Locke asserts that, because extrinsic denominations are not properties, they can change without a change occurring in the denominated thing, it would be altogether appropriate for Leibniz to respond that extrinsic denominations *are* properties of (or are included in) what they denominate, because as often as they change, a change *does* occur in the denominated thing. My reading of NPE is thus considerably more plausible in this regard than the reductionist view.

A further difficulty for reductionist NPE arises when we consider how one might derive it from IC. I am going to assume that the first move for the reductionist, or, indeed, for anyone else who attempts to reconstruct the argument, is to infer (9) from IC. (9) is a fairly immediate consequence of IC, and it is obviously a pertinent result when considering whether an extrinsic denomination can change without any change occurring in the denominated thing, which is a central point of dispute between Locke and Leibniz in this context. The challenge then facing a reductionist reconstruction of the IC argument is to explain how Leibniz might have reasoned to reductionist NPE from (9). The next move for the reductionist will likely be an assertion that Leibniz does not believe that extrinsic denominations are properties. That is, they will assert that Leibniz accepted (21). I believe this assertion is highly questionable as an interpretation of Leibniz. Whether or not it is something Leibniz accepted is a large part of what the debate over NPE is about and so a non-reductionist is certainly under no obligation to concede it to the reductionist so he can use it as a premise in an argument for a reductionist version of NPE. Nevertheless, as we will soon see, even if we do allow this assumption to the reductionist, the reductionist version of NPE still will not follow.

The reductionist reconstruction would then continue by observing that for a thing to change, one of its properties must change. And (9) informs us that whenever a thing's extrinsic denominations change, the thing changes as well. But if extrinsic denominations are not properties, then the change of extrinsic denomination cannot be constitutive of what has changed in the denominated thing. The thing would have to change with respect to one of its intrinsic denominations, since only they are genuine properties. Thus by (9) and (21)—and the assumption that a thing changes only if one of its properties changes—we have

(24) A change of extrinsic denomination is always accompanied by a change of intrinsic denomination.

Extrinsic Denominations and the Interconnection of All Things 63

And, with (24), it may appear that we are approaching what the reductionist is looking for, as (24) establishes a certain correlation between extrinsic denominations and intrinsic ones. But if we again recall that Leibniz is really only looking at type B changes of extrinsic denomination, we see that we are really nowhere near reductionist NPE. As discussed above, when (as a result of B taking on the property P, which A also has) A becomes similar to B, it is not A's having P that changes. Thus, whatever intrinsic denomination it is that changes in A, it is not one of the ones to which <similar to B> reduces. The intrinsic denomination of A that changes could seemingly be any number of things other than P. It could be that when A becomes similar to B, A grows an inch, or it could be that A develops a headache at precisely that moment. But it is not an intrinsic denomination that is relevant to a reduction of <similar to B>. Is there some way of going on from (24) to obtain reductionist NPE? I cannot see any, and, in any case, I cannot see any reason to even try. Once it is shown that, in type B cases, the intrinsic denomination that changes is not the one that (in the denominated individual at least) the extrinsic denomination reduces to, then what motivation could there possibly be to find a way of obtaining reductionist NPE? Once we reach (24), Locke's claim that because extrinsic denominations are not properties, they can change without a change in the denominated thing is successfully rebutted. What would drive us to the further claim that extrinsic denominations reduce to intrinsic ones when that claim is of no help in showing that Locke is wrong?

The reductionist could reject the construal I have placed on the Lockean context, and claim that Locke was actually attempting to derive (21) from (20), instead of the other way around. But I do not believe this would advance the reductionist case in any significant way. If Locke is reasoning from (20) to (21), then Leibniz's assertion of the IC principle together with its straightforward implication of (9) would appear to be an attack on the premise of Locke's argument. But Leibniz also offers NPE and so we must find a role for it to play in the response to Locke. The most natural function to ascribe to NPE in the argument would be that it presents some sort of a challenge to (21). At first glance, it may seem that reductionist NPE could be viewed as such a challenge. Reductionists could say that, though Leibniz shares Locke's belief that extrinsic denominations are not properties, he believes that this is not the whole of the matter. Though they are not properties, extrinsic denominations reduce to intrinsic denominations, which *are* properties. Leibniz's point in offering NPE is that Locke is oversimplifying things.

However, this approach is beset with the same sorts of difficulties as the preceding one. First of all, it may make minimal sense to assert some sort of reducibility thesis here, but not the reducibility thesis contained in reductionist NPE. In the IC argument for NPE, Leibniz is trying to show that the denominated thing changes even in type B cases. Given this context, if Leibniz *was* trying to prove the reducibility of extrinsic denominations to intrinsic ones, is it not fair to assume that he would by trying to show that the intrinsic denominations the extrinsic ones reduce to are the same ones that change when the denominated thing changes? And since, under reductionist NPE, the intrinsic denominations to which extrinsic denominations reduce are *not* the ones that change in type B cases, that would tend to show that Leibniz was not trying to establish reductionist NPE in this context. Second, as shown above, reductionist NPE does not follow from IC. IC, along with the highly contentious assumption that Leibniz did not believe extrinsic denominations are properties, only carries us as far as (24). And as (24) would suffice as a rebuttal to Locke, and since reductionist NPE is not anything Leibniz would have a reason to assert in this context, as it is useless in the context of type B changes, there are no grounds to go thrashing about the Leibnizian corpus in an attempt to find a premise(s) that will bridge the gap between (24) and reductionist NPE.

There is another serious difficulty with the view that reductionist NPE is the conclusion Leibniz has in mind in the IC argument. No matter how we construe the direction of the inferential connection between (20) and (21), Leibniz clearly sets forth NPE to counter Locke in *some* way. That is, NPE goes against *something* that Locke maintains. Yet the claim that whatever extrinsic denominations are true of a thing can be inferred from the intrinsic denominations of that thing and the intrinsic denominations of the thing to which it is related (i.e., reductionist NPE) is almost certainly a claim that Locke himself would endorse. On Locke's view relations and extrinsic denominations are not in things; they are results the mind reaches by comparing two things to each other in respect of one of their non-relational properties. The following remarks of Locke display a particularly reductionist flavor:

> And since any idea, whether simple, or complex, may be the occasion, why the mind thus brings two things together, and, as it were, takes a view of them at once, though still considered as distinct: therefore any of our ideas may be the foundation of relation.[29]

Thus, Locke says if one considers the whiteness of Caius and the whiteness of free-stone, one can infer that Caius is whiter than free-stone.[30] These statements together with Locke's explicit assertion that extrinsic denominations are not properties make a rather strong showing that Locke would have been in complete agreement with reductionist NPE. In fact, one can make a far better textual case that Locke was a reductionist than that Leibniz was. Therefore, I do not see how Leibniz can, with any plausibility, be understood as putting forth reductionist NPE as a rebuttal to Locke in the IC argument. Of course, Locke does not have the doctrine of the interconnection of all things, and so he accepts (20), and this remains a bone of contention between Locke and Leibniz. But Leibniz also clearly sets forth NPE as a point of opposition between himself and Locke, and reductionist NPE simply is not a claim that Locke would dispute. Again, reductionist NPE would just be the wrong thing for Leibniz to assert in response to Locke.

It appears, then, that regardless of whether Locke reasoned from (20) to (21) or from (21) to (20), reductionist NPE does not provide for a very plausible reconstruction of the IC argument. It is a claim that, in the context of his dispute with Locke, Leibniz seemingly would not want to make. And it does not follow from the premise Leibniz offers in the argument—the interconnection doctrine. What options remain for the reductionist view here? Cover and Hawthorne appear to adopt a rather novel approach to the argument. Their view seems to be that in order for Leibniz to maintain that extrinsic denominations are founded on intrinsic ones (i.e., reductionist NPE) and still account for type B cases of change, Leibniz must put forth a doctrine like the interconnection of all things. The claim that extrinsic denominations are founded on intrinsic ones does not by itself guarantee that the denominated thing will change, and so Leibniz must also maintain IC. This is precisely why according to them, Leibniz, in passages such as the one from the *New Essays* "connects" NPE with IC.[31] I agree that Leibniz needs IC if he is going to maintain reductionist NPE and still accept that each change of extrinsic denomination is accompanied by a real change in the denominated thing. But the obvious problem with this is that it simply does not fit Leibniz's reasoning in the IC argument. Leibniz does not argue that because NPE is true, IC is true. He argues in the opposite direction: because IC is true, then NPE is true. And once we have the argument pointed in the right direction, all of the above difficulties arise again. How does reductionist NPE *follow* from interconnection? Why would Leibniz even assert reductionist NPE in this context? What Cover and Hawthorne need to explain is how reductionist NPE can answer *these* questions.

VIII. Another Interpretation of NPE?

One possibility that naturally suggests itself here is that, since reductionist NPE appears to be an untenable interpretation in the context of the IC argument, and since (24)—if we assume extrinsic denominations are not properties—can be made to follow from IC, perhaps (24) itself could be what Leibniz meant by NPE. Perhaps Leibniz was not trying to show that extrinsic denominations *reduce* to intrinsic denominations, but only that extrinsic denominations are *correlated* with intrinsic denominations in such a way that any change of extrinsic denomination is accompanied by a change of intrinsic denomination (in the denominated thing). Such an interpretation certainly succeeds where the reductionist view fails in the setting of the IC argument. In addition to being something that can, with the high-powered yet questionable assistance of (21), follow from IC, (24) is also a statement that Leibniz could sensibly assert as a rebuttal to Locke. Despite this, I do not believe (24) provides a sound interpretation of NPE overall. It does not fit well in other contexts in which Leibniz asserts NPE. For instance, it would not be workable as a conclusion of the PS argument. Recall that, under (24), the intrinsic denominations with which extrinsic denominations are correlated could be anything. In type B cases of extrinsic denomination change, the intrinsic denomination that changes will not even be one from which we can infer the truth of the extrinsic denomination. How, then, could (24) follow from the PS principle? In the PS argument, Leibniz informs us that the PS principle is the basis of truth for propositions involving extrinsic denominations, and that NPE follows from this. I cannot see any way for the PS principle to drive us to an acceptance of (24). Presumably, such an argument would again invoke the claim that extrinsic denominations are not predicates and/or properties. So, propositions involving extrinsic denominations are not true because their predicates are included in their subjects.[32] Only propositions whose predicates are intrinsic denominations are true in this way. Therefore, propositions involving extrinsic denominations must be based in some way on propositions involving intrinsic ones. But, under (24), the intrinsic denominations upon which an extrinsic denomination is based may have no relevance to that extrinsic denomination. They are merely intrinsic denominations that change when the extrinsic ones with which they are correlated change. What has such a vague correlation to do with the truth of propositions involving extrinsic denominations? Nothing, it would seem, and thus (24), I believe, is not the result Leibniz was seeking. Furthermore, such loosely correlated intrinsic denominations could never serve as a foundation of or reason for propositions involving the extrinsic denominations with which they are correlated. Yet Leibniz explicitly concludes the PS argument with the claim that there are no purely extrinsic denominations which have no foundation in the thing denominated. (24) simply is not an interpretation of NPE that could ensure that extrinsic denominations have a foundation in the thing denominated.

IX. Another Reconstruction of the IC Argument for NPE Interpreted as (6)

Though I believe the interpretation of Locke that regards him as reasoning from (21) to (20) is the one that best fits his discussion, it is still conceivable that he intends to reason from (20) to (21). Thus, in this section, I offer a sketch of how the IC argument for NPE would be reconstructed against this

Extrinsic Denominations and the Interconnection of All Things 67

backdrop, and with NPE read as (6). First, my version of NPE is an appropriate thing for Leibniz to assert in response to Locke. Under this reading of Locke, Locke's point is that, since extrinsic denominations can change without a change occurring in the denominated thing, they are not properties of the denominated thing. Against this, Leibniz can well say, "But, in metaphysical strictness, they are properties of what they denominate" (i.e., my reading of NPE). Secondly, my version of NPE is the conclusion Leibniz would most likely draw from IC. As discussed earlier, IC clearly implies (9). And with (9), we know that the denominated thing changes whenever its extrinsic denominations do. Now this is supposed to imply something further about extrinsic denominations, and this something further is the NPE claim. I believe we can gain a worthwhile insight into what this further claim is if we consider the question of how a denominated thing can change whenever its extrinsic denominations change. There seem to be two ways the denominated thing could change whenever its extrinsic denominations do. I believe one of these two ways is what Leibniz means by NPE. The first way assumes that extrinsic denominations are not properties, and thus asserts that changes of extrinsic denomination are always accompanied by changes of intrinsic denomination, which is what (24) maintains. But, as argued above, this does not even begin to establish reductionist NPE. Moreover, reductionist NPE displays a poor fit with the IC argument in other ways. It makes no sense for Leibniz to assert it, since reductionist NPE fails to ensure that the denominated thing changes in type B cases. It also makes no sense for Leibniz to assert it as a rebuttal to Locke, because Locke arguably accepts reductionist NPE already. (24) as a reading of NPE is not plausible either. It works moderately well in the context of the IC argument (aside from its reliance on the claim that extrinsic denominations are not properties), but it does not work in other contexts in which Leibniz states NPE, such as the PS argument. Thus, neither reductionist NPE nor (24) constitute good answers to the question of what changes in the denominated thing when its extrinsic denominations change.

The other way that the denominated thing could change as often as its extrinsic denominations did would be if the change of extrinsic denomination *itself* constituted a change in the thing. Why would Leibniz believe that a change of extrinsic denomination was constitutive of a change in the denominated thing? This would actually be a natural thing for Leibniz to think in connection with type B cases. Leibniz is explicitly examining cases in which a change in my extrinsic denominations comes about "without any change in me, solely by change in the other person."[33] (9) demands that I change in such cases, but the only thing that has changed about me is one of my extrinsic denominations, and so the change of extrinsic denomination must constitute the change in me. And if that is so, then extrinsic denominations must be properties of the things denominated by them, for a change of extrinsic denomination would constitute a change in the denominated thing only if extrinsic denominations are properties.

One could respond that, though in a type B case the change of extrinsic denomination comes about solely because of a change in something else, this does not necessarily mean that the only thing that changes in the denominated thing is the extrinsic denomination itself. Because the extrinsic denomination <similar to B> becomes true of A as a result of B acquiring the property P, which A also has, does not mean that A's acquiring <similar to B> is the *only* thing that changes about A. It could be that when A becomes similar to B, A takes on the intrinsic denomination D, which, of course, has no relevance to whether or not <similar to B> is true of A, but is a change in A nonetheless. The only motivation I can see for Leibniz to believe that A takes on D is if he believed that extrinsic denominations were not properties. Why else would he appeal to such a thing to explain what had changed in A? However, it could also well be that the possibility of A's taking on some unrelated property D when he becomes similar to B never even occurred to Leibniz, which would render the assumption that the change of extrinsic denomination is all that has changed in A quite natural. Thus, depending on what assumed premises are supplied, the argument could lead to (24) or it could lead to my version of NPE. If we assume that extrinsic denominations are not properties, (24) follows from (9). If we assume that the only thing that changes in type B cases is the extrinsic denomination itself, then my view follows. My view is very much to be preferred over (24), though. For (24) simply is not a plausible reading of NPE in the context of the PS argument. Whereas my view works extremely well in that context.

Chapter Five

Extrinsic Denominations and the Foundations of Relations

I. Introduction

This chapter has two aims. The first is to provide a textually responsible, non-reductionist account of Leibniz's claim that extrinsic denominations are founded on intrinsic denominations. The second is to explain the connection of NPE to this claim. With regard to the first aim, I argue that when Leibniz asserts that extrinsic denominations are founded on intrinsic ones, the surrounding context nearly always makes clear that he is merely asserting that relations simpliciter are founded on intrinsic denominations. I further argue that the intrinsic denominations upon which relations simpliciter are founded are actually relational accidents. This, of course, requires a showing that relational accidents can be plausibly regarded as intrinsic denominations. Leibniz frequently uses the term "extrinsic denomination" to refer to denominations that are extrinsic to or out of what they denominate, and relations simpliciter are extrinsic denominations in just this sense. In keeping with this, intrinsic denominations are those that are in or intrinsic to what they denominate, and as Leibniz considers relational accidents to be in things, they are intrinsic denominations in this sense. This showing points the way to an understanding of how NPE is related to the claim that extrinsic denominations are founded on intrinsic denominations. NPE, under my interpretation, is the claim that there are no extrinsic denominations (where "extrinsic denomination" is here understood as a relational accident) that are not in what they denominate. And so, because denominations that are in what they denominate are rightly counted as intrinsic denominations, NPE is basically the assertion that what are commonly considered extrinsic denominations are actually intrinsic denominations. Thus, NPE must be true for relations simpliciter to have their foundations in things. This is precisely the result Leibniz seeks to establish in his essay, *On the Principle of Indiscernibles*. Leibniz argues that because a thing's position in space, which is a relation simpliciter, requires a foundation in things, NPE must be true. The central premise of this argument is the famous principle of the identity of indiscernibles.

70 Leibniz on Denominations

Hence, in this chapter, the opportunity of considering Leibniz's third argument for NPE arises. As with the PS and IC arguments, the approach I take is that of comparative reconstruction. I argue that my reading of NPE is a far more plausible candidate for the conclusion of this argument than its reductionist counterpart.

II. A Reductionist Proof Text?

Leibniz does indeed claim more than once that extrinsic denominations are founded on intrinsic ones. As mentioned in chapter one, two of the passages most commonly cited by reductionists are:

> To be in a place is not a bare extrinsic denomination; indeed, there is no denomination so extrinsic that it does not have an intrinsic denomination as its basis.[1]

> In general, place, position and quantity, such as number and proportion, are merely relations, and result from other things which by themselves either constitute or terminate a change . . . .[T]hey are mere results, which do not constitute any intrinsic denomination per se, and so they are merely relations which demand a foundation from the category of quality, that is, from an intrinsic accidental denomination.[2]

These passages present an undeniably reductionist appearance. That is, it seems that the reductionist reading of NPE provides a natural interpretation of these passages. For under that reading, extrinsic denominations are not properties. If a given extrinsic denomination is true of A, then that it is true of A can be inferred from the intrinsic denominations of A and the intrinsic denominations of the thing to which the extrinsic denomination relates A. This view of the relationship between extrinsic and intrinsic denominations would appear to be a perfectly natural way of understanding the claim that extrinsic denominations are founded on intrinsic ones. And if this is *not* what Leibniz means, then how should we understand that claim? In particular, if, as I maintain, Leibniz regards extrinsic denominations as properties of the thing denominated, then why does he say they are founded on intrinsic denominations? What could such a claim mean under a view like mine?

III. The Solution

My basic answer to this problem is that whenever Leibniz speaks of extrinsic denominations being founded upon intrinsic ones, he is using "extrinsic denomination" to refer to what I have been calling relations simpliciter. Leibniz, as discussed in chapter one, distinguishes relations simpliciter from relational accidents, and he accords differing statuses to each. Because they violate the doctrine of individual accidents, relations simpliciter cannot be accidents of things, whereas Leibniz appears to assert that relational accidents *are* legitimate accidents of things. If relations simpliciter are the extrinsic denominations that Leibniz claims are founded on intrinsic denominations, then that would pose no problem for my view whatsoever. So long as Leibniz countenances relational accidents as genuine accidents the claim that relations simpliciter are founded on intrinsic denominations is not adverse to my view in any way.

When Leibniz speaks of relations or extrinsic denominations being founded on intrinsic ones, the examples he uses, or other features of the surrounding context, generally make it clear that he is only asserting that relations simpliciter are founded on intrinsic denominations. Consider, first of all, the above two passages. Both of the passages discuss the example of place. The first passage declares place to be an extrinsic denomination that is founded on intrinsic denominations. The second passage refers to place as a "mere relation" that is founded upon intrinsic denominations. But, for Leibniz, place is the example *par excellence* of a relation simpliciter. To see that this is so we must take a brief look at Leibniz's account of the nature of space. Leibniz famously held that space is not an absolute entity that exists apart from the things in it, as though it were a container which contained everything in existence.[3] Nor is it a property of things that occupy space.[4] Rather, space is relative:

> I have said more than once that I hold space to be something merely relative, as time is, that I hold it be an order of coexistences, as time is an order of successions. . . . And when many things are seen together, one perceives that order of things among themselves.[5]

The quote indicates that Leibniz regards space as an order of coexistence. This order of coexistence is an order that the objects in space display in relation to one another, and the order Leibniz has in mind is essentially the distance of the objects from one another or their situations with respect to one another.

> This is how men come to form the notion of space. They consider that several things exist at the same time, and they find in them a certain order of co-existence, in accordance with which the relation of one thing to another is more or less simple. This is their situation or distance.[6]

Thus space is relative in the sense that it is simply the relations of distance or situation that objects stand in to one another. Now, a place is a particular location in space. And the relations of situation or distance are what determine a thing's place.

> To give a kind of definition: Place is that which is said to be the same for A and for B, when the relation of co-existence between B and C, E, F, G, etc., entirely agrees with the relation of co-existence which A previously had with those bodies, supposing there has been no cause of change in C, E, F, G, etc.[7]

To be in a place is nothing more that to stand at certain distances from objects that are assumed to remain fixed. If A moves, while C, E, F, G, etc. remain fixed, and B comes to have the same relations of situation to C, E, F, G, etc., as A had, then B has taken A's place.

Yet, though place is to be understood in this way, Leibniz cautions that we must not identify place with relations of situation, as the two have differing ontological statuses.

> And it is well here to consider the difference between place and the relation of situation of the body which occupies the place. For the place of A and B is the same, whereas the relation of A to fixed bodies is not precisely and individually the same as the relation that B (which is to take its place) will have to the same fixed bodies; these relations only agree. For two different subjects, such as A and B, cannot have exactly the same individual affection, since one and the same individual accident cannot occur in two subjects, nor pass from one subject to another. But the mind, not content with agreement, seeks an identity, a thing which is truly the same, and conceives it as outside these subjects; and this is what is here called *place* and *space*. This, however, can only be ideal, comprising a certain order wherein the mind conceives the application of the relations.[8]

The passage makes a number of important points. First, it explicitly asserts that relations of situation are genuine accidents of things. Leibniz goes out of his way to say that, though B takes A's place and thus takes on the relations of situation to fixed bodies that A formerly had, the relations of situation that B now has to fixed bodies only agree with those that A had. Leibniz does not explain what sort of agreement he intends here. It is clear from the passage that the agreement relation involves a very strong similarity between the things that agree, because B, in order to take A's place, must stand at the same distance from the fixed bodies as A once did. But the passage also makes clear that agreement is weaker than identity. At any rate, the precise nature of the agreement is not crucial here. What is crucial is that, for Leibniz, because these relations of situation only agree, they do not violate the doctrine of individual accidents, and so they can be genuine relational accidents of A and B successively. If Leibniz did not think relations of situation were genuine accidents, then why does he say that, since "one and the same individual accident cannot occur in two subjects, nor pass from one subject to another," these relations only agree? The only reason he could have to argue this way is that he believes these relations of situation are accidents that inhere in things.

Yet, though the relations of situation of A and B only agree, the resulting place of A and B is truly identical. And it is for this reason that place is a relation simpliciter. If the place of A and B is truly identical, then if place were an accident it would be an accident that is passed from A to B when A moves and B assumes A's place. Yet it is part of the doctrine of individual accidents that the *same* accident cannot "pass from one subject to another." Place is thus a "mere relation."

A mere few sentences following the above passage on the difference between place and relations of situation, Leibniz writes these words:

> I will give another example of the mind's habit of creating for itself, upon occasion of accidents existing in subjects, something which corresponds to those accidents outside the subjects The ratio or proportion between two lines L and M may be conceived in three ways: as a ratio of the greater L to the lesser M, as a ratio of the lesser M to the greater L, and, lastly, as something abstracted from both, that is, the ratio between L and M without considering which is the antecedent or which the consequent, which the subject and which the object....In the first way of considering, L the greater, in the second, M the lesser, is the subject of that accident which philosophers call "relation." But which of them will be the subject in the third way of considering them? It cannot be said that both of them, L and M together, are the subject of such an accident; for, if so, we should have an accident in two subjects, one with one leg in one and the other in the other....Therefore we must say that this relation, in this third way of considering it, is indeed out of the subjects; but being neither a substance nor an accident, it must be a mere mental thing, the consideration of which is nevertheless useful.[9]

The first sentence of this passage further underscores the fact that in the preceding example, the one involving place and relations of situation, Leibniz is asserting that place is a relation simpliciter, while relations of situation are genuine relational accidents "existing in subjects." Moreover, this latter example demonstrates that Leibniz regarded bare ratios or proportions as relations simpliciter. Returning again to the two earlier quoted passages in which Leibniz asserts that extrinsic denominations/relations are founded on intrinsic denominations, in the second of those, Leibniz refers to proportion as a mere relation that is founded on intrinsic denominations. Therefore, Leibniz's assertion that proportion is founded on intrinsic denominations is only a claim that a certain relation simpliciter is founded on intrinsic denominations.

This showing is not limited to the relations simpliciter of place and proportion. In a passage from Leibniz's correspondence with des Bosses, Leibniz says

> I do not believe that you will admit an accident that is in two subjects at the same time. My judgment about relations is that paternity in David is one thing,

sonship in Solomon another, but that the relation common to both is a merely mental thing *whose foundation is the modifications of the individuals.*[10]

The structure of the passage closely parallels the structure of the two preceding passages. Both paternity and sonship are very plausibly reckoned as relational accidents, and Leibniz declares that they are "in" their respective subjects. But the relation common to both is founded on the modifications of individuals. But the passage concerns more than just Leibniz's view of the paternal relations between David and Solomon. Leibniz is offering his general "judgement about relations"; the case of David and Solomon is merely an instance of that general view. Leibniz expressly and repeatedly declares that relational accidents are real accidents, while relations simpliciter are mere mental entities that are founded on intrinsic denominations. Hence, Leibniz's claim that extrinsic denominations/relations are founded on intrinsic denominations is not adverse to my view in the least.

IV. What Are Relations Simpliciter Founded On?

I have thus far not considered the question of what intrinsic denominations relations simpliciter are founded on. It would be easy to assume that Leibniz has strictly non-relational denominations in mind here. And it would, of course, do no harm to my view if that were how Leibniz views the matter. It really does not matter if extrinsic denominations are based upon non-relational denominations, so long as Leibniz understands extrinsic denominations as relations simpliciter in these passages. I do not believe, however, that non-relational denominations are what Leibniz has in view here. I believe passages like the above suggest that it is the relational accidents themselves that relations simpliciter are based on. It would surely be natural to regard place as being founded upon relations of situation, for, as Leibniz makes clear, being in a place is really nothing more than standing in certain distance relations to fixed bodies. Leibniz himself describes this as an "example of the mind's habit of creating for itself, upon occasion of accidents existing *in* subjects, something which *corresponds* to those accidents outside the subjects" [emphasis added]. Relations simpliciter "correspond" to the relational accidents, and I believe we can understand this correspondence as the former being founded upon the latter. Surprisingly, even reductionists, such as Mates and Cover and Hawthorne, acknowledge that it is the relational accidents that provide the basis of relations simpliciter.[11] They are quick to distance themselves from the apparent anti-reductionist implications of their admission, however, by claiming that the relational accidents ultimately reduce to non-relational ones. I will examine this claim shortly, but for now I only wish to note that even reductionists believe Leibniz founds relations simpliciter, at least initially, on relational accidents.

Extrinsic Denominations and the Foundations of Relations   75

We have seen that when Leibniz speaks of extrinsic denominations as being founded upon intrinsic denominations he is speaking of relations simpliciter being founded on intrinsic denominations. And it has also now been asserted that relational accidents are the foundation of relations simpliciter. Does this mean that Leibniz is referring to relational accidents as intrinsic denominations? I believe the answer is Yes. There is a clear trend in Leibniz's usage of "extrinsic denomination" and "intrinsic denomination" that suggests he sometimes applies the former term to denominations that are *out of* or extrinsic to what they denominate, and the latter term to refer to denominations that are *in* or intrinsic to what they denominate. Thus, if, as Leibniz seems clearly to maintain, relational accidents are *in* substances, they can be intrinsic denominations in just that sense. The following two passages illustrate Leibniz's use of "extrinsic denomination" to designate a denomination that is out of what it denominates and "intrinsic denomination" to designate a denomination that is in what it denominates.

> For I ask whether this volition or command, or if you prefer, this divine law once established, has bestowed upon things only an extrinsic denomination or whether it has truly conferred upon them some created impression which endures within them.[12]

> Suppose for instance that the imaginary 'Australians' swarmed into our latitudes: it is likely that some way would be found of distinguishing them from us; but if not, and if God had forbidden the mingling of these races, and if Jesus Christ had redeemed only our own, then we should have to try to introduce artificial marks to distinguish the races from one another. No doubt there would be an inner difference, but since we should be unable to detect it we should have to rely solely on the extrinsic denomination of birth, and try to associate with it an indelible artificial mark which would provide an intrinsic denomination and a permanent means of telling our race apart from theirs[13]

(The second passage's mention of "the extrinsic denomination of birth" refers to *place* of birth, and is thus another instance of Leibniz calling place an extrinsic denomination.) And in the Arnauld Correspondence, Leibniz asserts that, because of the PS doctrine of truth, any predicate that is true of a subject is "intrinsic" to that subject.[14] Elsewhere in the *Correspondence,* as discussed in chapter two, Leibniz says that PS leads to the inclusion of extrinsic denominations in complete individual concepts.[15] Such included extrinsic denominations can then fairly be said to be intrinsic denominations in the sense that they are intrinsic to the concept of the things they denominate. It is therefore quite consistent with Leibniz's usage of "extrinsic denomination" and "intrinsic denomination" for him to assert that extrinsic denominations are founded on intrinsic denominations and mean that relations simpliciter are founded on relational properties.

76 Leibniz on Denominations

If extrinsic denominations are so-called because they are out of what they denominate, then it would be quite natural to construe the claim that there are no purely extrinsic denominations as the claim that there are no denominations (that truly denominate the thing) that are out of what they denominate. In other words, NPE would be the claim that all true denominations are in what they denominate. Of course, this is essentially the interpretation of NPE I am defending here. But Leibniz sometimes refers to relations simpliciter as extrinsic denominations, and so if NPE means what I say, that would seem to imply that relations simpliciter are in things as well. My response to this is that NPE only applies to extrinsic denominations that are relational properties; it does not apply to extrinsic denominations that are relations simpliciter. Such a response naturally appears *ad hoc*, and this would present an advantage to the reductionist, for the reductionist believes both bare relations and relational properties reduce to non-relational properties. There is, however, a very principled reason to restrict NPE's application to relational properties: Leibniz, as we have seen, explicitly advocates different treatment for relations simpliciter and relational properties. He declares the former to be merely mental, while the latter are really in things. Yet though he regards the two differently, he carelessly refers to both as relations in some passages,[16] and in other passages he refers to what are clearly relations simpliciter, such as place and ratio, as extrinsic denominations.[17] But in other places he seems, appropriately, to distinguish relations from extrinsic denominations.[18] So, given the unruly textual situation with regard to these terms and in particular that Leibniz sometimes refers to both relations simpliciter and relational properties as extrinsic denominations, and given also that he considers one to be ideal and the other to be a genuine property, it is not at all surprising that we should have to impose a restriction on the sort of extrinsic denominations to which NPE may apply. I hold, then, that NPE is only the claim that there are no relational properties of a thing that are not included in (the concept of) that thing.

V. NPE and The Foundations of Relations

That Leibniz regards relations simpliciter as founded on relational accidents suggests that the NPE doctrine could be relevant to the founding of relations. And in an essay entitled, *On the Principle of Indiscernibles*, Leibniz does indeed relate the two doctrines to one another. Leibniz argues that because relations simpliciter require a foundation in the things related, then NPE must be true. NPE's being true is what will provide relations simpliciter with the requisite foundation in things. To show this, Leibniz considers the relations simpliciter of place and time (though most of what he says only concerns place), and his aim is to show that the relational accidents with which they are correlated

Extrinsic Denominations and the Foundations of Relations 77

(e.g., the relations of situation, in the case of place) are genuine accidents. Leibniz states his argument as follows:

> A consideration which is of the greatest importance in all philosophy, and in theology itself, is this: there are no purely extrinsic denominations, because . . . . it is not possible for two things to differ from one another in respect of place and time alone, but that it is always necessary that there shall be some other internal difference . . . .For all things which are different must be distinguished in some way, and in the case of real things position alone is not a sufficient means of distinction.[19]

Leibniz is here concerned with ruling out the possibility that two things could be alike in every respect but occupy different locations in space. Because of his acceptance of the identity of indiscernibles (hereafter referred to as ID) Leibniz cannot countenance such a possibility. As we have seen, a thing's position is not an accident of that thing, and so if two distinct things were alike in every respect but occupied different spatial locations, they would not differ with respect to any genuine property, and this would violate the ID principle. In this argument, Leibniz formulates ID as: "all things which are different must be distinguished in some way." That is, if two things A and B are truly distinct, then there will be some property, P, which one has and the other lacks.[20] Since a thing's position cannot serve as such a distinguishing property, then two things which are truly distinct must differ in some other respect, with respect to something that is a genuine property. Now, given only this much information, it might seem that any property would do. If two things differ in place, then as long as they differ in some respect, ID will be preserved. In one situation, it could be that one of the things is blue, while the other is not; in another it could be that one is human and the other is not, and so on. It would not really matter how they differ, just as long as they did. But I do not think Leibniz had anything this loose in mind. What he wants to show here, rather, is that the difference in place *itself* guarantees that there will be a difference in the properties of the two things. That is, Leibniz wants to show that, though place itself is not a property, it is founded upon things that are properties, and so if two things differ in place, they will differ with regard to the foundations of their respective places. For Leibniz goes on in the essay to say,

> To be in a place seems, abstractly at any rate, to imply nothing but position. But in actuality, that which has a place must express place in itself; so that distance and the degree of distance involves also a degree of expressing in the thing itself a remote thing . . . .[W]e conceive position as something extrinsic, which adds nothing to the thing posited, though it does add the way in which it is affected by other things.[21]

Since, as this passage makes clear, place expresses itself in the thing occupying the place, then two things that differ in place will have different expressions of place within themselves, and so they will differ from one another. Place adds to a thing the way that thing is affected by other things. Therefore, it is not that Leibniz thinks that two things that differ in place will differ in just any respect. The difference between them will arise directly from their difference in place.

How is it, exactly, that place adds to a thing the way that thing is affected by other things? Leibniz's descriptions of this in the essay are fairly cryptic, but I believe it is through the relations of situation (from which place arises) that place makes its addition. Leibniz never offers an example of a relation of situation either, but it is clear that it involves a thing's distance from another thing. For present purposes, I believe it will suffice to regard a relation of situation as being a relational property of roughly the form <x feet from A> (where "x" is a non-negative number and "A" is an individual). This may well be an oversimplified description of a relation of situation. However, it is enough for now that being in a place involves having a set of relational properties of roughly the form just described. For having such properties provides a reasonable construction of how place adds to a thing the way that thing is affected by other things, or how distance involves expressing in the thing itself a remote thing. We know that, according to Leibniz's theory of space, to be in a place is nothing more than standing in certain relations of situation to fixed coexistents. These relations of situation are relational properties that refer to a thing's distance from other things. So, if being in a place adds to a thing affectations from other things, or if distance involves expressing a remote thing, then a natural choice for how this occurs is through the thing's relations of situation.

With this understanding of how a place expresses itself in the thing that occupies that place, we are now in a position to understand how a difference in place between two things can give rise to a difference in the properties of those two things, even though place itself is not a property. Recall that Leibniz maintains that two things (successively) occupy the same place if their relations of situation to fixed coexistents agree. It follows from this that if two things differ in place, then their relations of situation to fixed coexistents will also differ.[22] Now, there are seemingly two ways that a difference in the relations of situation could result in a difference in the properties of the two things. If relations of situation are themselves genuine properties, then two things that differ in place will have different properties—viz., they will have differing relations of situation. Alternatively, if it is presumed that relations of situation are not properties, then, if relations of situation reduce to things that are properties, two things that differ in place could have different properties. The former scenario is, of course, the one that corresponds to my reading of NPE, while the latter corresponds to the reductionist reading of NPE. I will discuss the plausibility of each of these shortly. For now, I only wish to point out that in the ID argument for NPE, it is the requirement that place have a foundation in things that is supposed to drive us to NPE. The argument takes ID as true. If two things are distinct, then there must be a difference in the properties of the two. Obviously, if two things differ in place, then they are distinct from each other. Leibniz wants to show that it is not so much as possible for two things to differ in place without also differing in their properties. Thus, place must have a foundation in the thing occupying that place, so that a difference in place itself will entail a difference in properties. And it is from this that Leibniz infers NPE. That place must have a foundation in the thing requires that NPE be true, since only if NPE is true will place have its foundation. I believe even reductionists would agree with the reconstruction of the argument up to this point. I also believe they will agree that place acquires its foundation in things through the relations of situation. But it is after this point that the reductionist and I part company.

On my view, showing that relations of situation are genuine properties is the result Leibniz is seeking in the ID argument. That is, Leibniz's point is that because place must have a foundation in things, the relations of situation from which place arises must be in things. And that relations of situation are genuine properties is what NPE, read as (6)—i.e., there are no extrinsic denominations of a thing that are not included in the concept of that thing— would maintain with regard to relations of situation.[23] This reading has a strong textual consideration in its favor. In the earlier quoted passage in which Leibniz distinguishes place from relations of situation, Leibniz expressly declares that relations of situation are genuine accidents. Leibniz goes out of his way to say even though two things (successively) occupy the same place, their relations of situation only agree, because two things cannot have the same accident, even in succession. They can only have accidents that agree. This is nothing less than a somewhat roundabout way of saying that relations of situation are accidents that inhere in things. And Leibniz's subsequent example involving the lengths of L and M further confirms this (see pp. 73 above). There are, as we have seen in section III, solid textual grounds for the claim that Leibniz regarded relations simpliciter, of which place is an example, as founded on relational accidents. It is therefore plausible to believe that Leibniz is attempting to prove that relations of situation are in things in the ID argument. That relations of situation are in things means that they can be regarded as intrinsic denominations, and so the demand that place be founded upon intrinsic denominations is met.

For reductionists, NPE, as applied to relations of situation, is not an assertion that relations of situation are genuine properties. Instead, it is the claim that relations of situation reduce to things that are properties. Reductionists will agree that place gains its foothold in things via relations of situation, but the relations of situation themselves reduce to non-relational properties. Thus, place ultimately has its foundation in non-relational properties of things. But the same textual considerations that commended my reading of NPE above undermine the reductionist claim. If Leibniz means to assert the reducibility of relations of situation, then why does he elsewhere say they are accidents of things? Again, he declares that place is indeed out of things because allowing it to be in things violates the doctrine of individual accidents. Relations of situation, on the other hand, *are* accidents. Given that Leibniz says this, it is hard to believe that he is here attempting to prove their reducibility.

Cover and Hawthorne attempt to provide an explanation of Leibniz's claim that relational accidents are in things that is consistent with reductionism. According to them, when Leibniz states that relational accidents are in things, what he means is that the non-relational accidents that provide the foundation for relational accidents are in things.[24] Commenting on the earlier quoted passage concerning the paternity and filiation relations that obtain between David and Solomon (see p. 73–74 above), they say,

> Part of the point of the quoted passage is to underscore the fact that, for Leibniz, as for the scholastics, a healthy first step when confronted with a relational claim—in this case "*a* is the father of *b*"—is to analyze it into two relational predications, one concerning *a*, another concerning *b*, with the two-place relation being treated as a merely mental construction. For us ... this is but the first stage in a fully reductive analysis whereby only intrinsic accidents lie at the ground floor.[25]

The passage makes clear that, for them, relations simpliciter are, at least initially, founded on relational accidents, as reducing relations simpliciter to relational accidents is the "first step" in the analysis. This supports my claim that reductionists will agree that in the ID argument Leibniz is attempting to found place on relations of situation. But, according to them, such a founding is only the *first* step. On what grounds, though, can this founding of relations simpliciter on relational accidents be characterized as merely the first step? In no passage does Leibniz ever carry the reduction any further. Why, then, should we believe that he nevertheless believed the "reduction" went further?

One consideration that Cover and Hawthorne seem to offer in support of their characterization is that if Leibniz really meant for the analysis of the relation simpliciter to terminate at relational accidents, then the analysis would be trivial.[26] It would be extremely uninformative for Leibniz to analyze the paternal relation between David and Solomon into the relational accidents "father of Solomon" and "son of David," and then stop. Now, I agree that such an analysis is rather unenlightening, but there is a question I would like to ask about Cover and Hawthorne's charge: at exactly what point did the task become one of giving an analysis? In the ID argument, Leibniz is only seeking to prove that two things cannot differ with respect to place alone, and so place must have a foundation in things. He quite simply has no need of an "analysis" of place to accomplish this. And in no other passage in which he distinguishes relations simpliciter from relational accidents does he even vaguely hint that his aim is to provide an analysis of relations simpliciter. Since there is no reason to think Leibniz wanted to provide an analysis in these passages in the first place, there are no grounds to complain that unless we carry the alleged analysis further, it will be trivial.

Are there any other considerations that might underwrite the first-step characterization? Perhaps if, as Cover and Hawthorne maintain, allowing relational accidents really did violate the doctrine of individual accidents, then we would have grounds for thinking that, despite the fact that Leibniz never goes any further in his "reductions," he did mean these to be first steps in a fully reductive analysis, as he would never have allowed relational accidents. But, as was shown in chapter three, Cover and Hawthorne's claim that allowing relational accidents would violate the doctrine of individual accidents is implausible. So that will not do. Are there any other passages that might lead one to think Leibniz did not view relational accidents as legitimate accidents? There are, as we have seen, numerous passages in which Leibniz says that extrinsic denominations are included in complete individual concepts and that relational accidents are in things, but there are none in which he asserts the opposite. And the passages in which Leibniz claims that extrinsic denominations are founded on intrinsic denominations are only assertions that relations simpliciter are founded on relational accidents. And once this is understood, such passages actually cut against the reductionist view, for they strongly suggest that relational accidents are intrinsic to the things whose accidents they are.

Cover and Hawthorne's assertion that these passages contain but the first step of a complete reduction of relations to non-relational accidents thus appears to be altogether without merit. And, as this was the move they would have to make to motivate a reductionist reconstruction of the ID argument for NPE, the reductionist reconstruction of that argument is similarly lacking in merit. There is simply no reason to suppose that Leibniz was trying to show the reducibility of relations of situation in the ID argument when he elsewhere claims that they are accidents in things. The reconstruction of the argument that sees it as an attempt to prove that the relations of situation are genuine accidents clearly fits far better with that claim.

Chapter Six

Extrinsic Denominations and the Claim that Every Monad Expresses the Universe

I. Introduction

In this chapter, I examine NPE's role as a premise in an argument that Leibniz offers to establish his famous claim that every monad expresses or mirrors the universe. The approach of this chapter, as in the previous ones, will be to reconstruct the argument both with NPE read as (6) and with it read reductionistically. Consideration of the argument is complicated by the fact that its conclusion—that every monad expresses the universe—is itself not entirely clear. It is relatively certain from Leibniz's writings that in order for a monad to express the universe, one must be able to infer from that monad's properties every property of every other monad in that universe. What is not so clear is how the monad's properties permit one to obtain this vast amount of information. The fact that Leibniz argues from NPE to the doctrine of expression suggests that a monad's extrinsic denominations, in some manner, play a vital role in its expression of the universe. It could be that if extrinsic denominations are genuine properties of what they denominate, then, since those denominations have the complete concepts of other individuals as components, one could obtain complete information about those other individuals simply by examining the extrinsic denominations of a single individual. This is, of course, in keeping with my reading of NPE and, as will be seen, is central to my rendering of how Leibniz derives expression from NPE. On the other hand, for a reductionist, although a monad's extrinsic denominations are crucially involved in its expression of the universe, they are not involved by being genuine properties of what they denominate. It seems, rather, that they would be involved in expression because they reduce to features of a thing that are genuine properties, and this is presumably how the reductionist version of NPE might imply monadic expression.

The focus of this chapter will be to determine which view of NPE leads more plausibly to the doctrine of expression. In section II, I present Leibniz's descriptions of the general notion of expression and discuss some of the interpretations of that notion given by interpreters. In section III, I discuss two features of monadic expression that are relevant to reconstructing the argument from NPE to monadic expression. The first is that monads do express the universe in some way through their extrinsic denominations. The second is that even though monads express the universe via their extrinsic denominations, they do not do so by simply containing the concepts of other individuals in their own concepts. Then, in section IV, I offer a reconstruction of the argument with NPE read as (6). I argue that if NPE is viewed this way, a version of monadic expression that displays the above two features follows immediately. In the final section, I consider how the argument fares under the reductionist view. Using Robert Sleigh's reductionist treatment of the argument as a model, I conclude that monadic expression cannot be plausibly inferred from the reductionist version of NPE.

II. Expression in General

The following are the principal texts in which Leibniz provides a general characterization of expression:

> That is said to express a thing in which there are relations which correspond to the relations of the thing expressed. But there are various kinds of expression; for example, the model of a machine expresses the machine itself, the projective delineation on a plane expresses a solid, speech expresses thoughts and truths, characters express numbers, and an algebraic equation expresses a circle of some other figure. What is common to all these expressions is that we can pass from a consideration of the relations in the expression to a knowledge of the corresponding properties of the thing expressed.[1]

> One thing expresses another, in my usage, when there is a constant and regular relation between what can be said about one about the other.[2]

> For it is sufficient for the expression of one thing in another that there should be a certain constant relational law, by which particulars in the one can be referred to corresponding particulars in the other.[3]

It is clear from the passages (especially the first) that if one thing expresses another, then one can, by considering the properties or relations of the expressing thing, determine the properties of the expressed thing. And this can happen because a "constant and regular relation" or "relational law" exists between the relations of one and the properties of the other. Interpreters have differed, though, over how this relational law should be understood. Some have claimed that the nature of the relational law is that of an isomorphism between expression and expressed thing.[4] But, as Chris Swoyer has pointed out, if the nature of the isomorphism is understood in the technical sense of a one-to-one mapping from the attributes of one thing onto another that preserves all of the structure of the first, then it is very unlikely to have been what Leibniz had in mind.[5] For certain of Leibniz's instances of expression (e.g., speech's expression of thought), as they almost certainly defy one-to-one mapping, do not meet the requirements for an isomorphism. Thus, most interpreters maintain that, for Leibniz, a mapping weaker than that required for isomorphism suffices for expression.[6]

Just how short this mapping can fall of being an isomorphism is also disputed, however. For example, Mates claims that expression requires, "only that from features of the expression it should be possible to derive, by some sort of calculation based on a law, features of the thing expressed."[7] Under this highly abstract characterization of expression, so long as there was some function which took as inputs the attributes of one thing and yielded as outputs the attributes of another, the first could be said to express the second. The two things would not have to be alike at all. By contrast, Swoyer has argued that in order for one thing to express another, there must be a mapping from (either) one to the other that preserves at least some of the structure of the expressing thing.[8]

I will forego rendering an opinion as to which, if any, of the non-isomorphic accounts of expression is correct. As nearly as I can tell, nothing I say in what follows will presuppose the correctness of any of these accounts, nor will what I say conflict with any of them. My primary interest here is with the expression relationship that obtains between monads and the universe, and, above all, with how Leibniz derives the existence of this relationship from NPE. The view of monadic expression that I claim Leibniz infers from NPE appears to satisfy even the more stringent general (non-isomorphic) accounts of expression, and therefore satisfies the less demanding ones as well. In addition, the objections I intend to raise against the reductionist view will, I believe, tell against it regardless of which general account of expression is adopted.[9]

III. Monadic Expression

In this section I would like to bring to the fore some of the particular features of monadic expression that I believe will figure prominently in reconstructing the NPE argument for monadic expression. A monad expresses or "mirrors" its universe by expressing all of the other monads that inhabit its universe.[10] As monadic expression is a species of general expression, to say that each monad expresses every other means that by considering the features of a single monad, a mind of sufficient capacity could determine the features of every other.[11] Now, a number a Leibniz's pronouncements on monadic expression make clear that a monad's relations to other monads and/or its extrinsic denominations, play a vital role in its expression of other monads. In addition to the first of the three passages on general expression quoted above, Leibniz says in section 56 of *Monadology* that

> This connection or adaptation of all created things with each, and of each with all the rest, means that each simple substance has relations which express all the others, and that consequently it is a perpetual living mirror of the universe.[12]

Additionally, the very fact that Leibniz argues from NPE to monadic expression indicates that some fact about extrinsic denominations (viz., whatever it is that NPE asserts) implies that monads express the universe. We must therefore attempt to determine how it is exactly that a monad's extrinsic denominations are involved in its expression of every other monad.

One natural way to understand the role of extrinsic denominations in expression is that monads simply contain such denominations in their individual concepts (and/or the corresponding relational accidents in themselves). And as the complete individual concepts of other monads are components of these denominations one could determine the attributes of other monads simply by examining these denominations.[13] As will become evident when I reconstruct the NPE argument for expression in line with my interpretation of NPE, such a picture is, roughly, how I see the role of extrinsic denominations in expression.

This account of extrinsic denominations' involvement in expression will clearly not be acceptable to reductionists, however. A reductionist simply would not accept the inclusion of extrinsic denominations in individual concepts or of relational accidents in monads. But then the reductionist must find another way to explain the role of extrinsic denominations in expression. What does Leibniz mean when he says that "each simple substance has relations which express all the others"? How does the reductionist reading of NPE imply that monadic expression occurs? With regard to the first of these questions, a reductionist is likely to claim that when Leibniz speaks of a substance having relations, he does not mean that substances have relations as accidents. Rather, he means merely that substances stand in relations to other substances. And that each substance is related to all the others allows them to express the others because these relations, though they are not themselves accidents, reduce to features of the substance which are. This is the point at which the reductionist version of NPE is likely to enter the picture. Somehow the fact that the relations reduce to non-relational attributes of monads opens the door for each monad to express all of the others. Whether the specific sort of reduction that reductionists speak of can plausibly imply expression is something I will take up in section V below. Nevertheless, I believe that the foregoing reasonably approximates the way reductionists will view the role of extrinsic denominations in expression, and also, as will be seen, approximates a reductionist reconstruction of the NPE argument for expression.

Another important aspect of monadic expression is that a monad does not express the others by simply containing the complete individual concepts of the others in its concept. In an important passage from his correspondence with de Volder, Leibniz states

> Who will deny, too, that one substance is modified by the intervention of another, as when a body is repelled by some obstacle in its path? In order to conceive the rebound of one of these bodies, therefore, the concept of both of them will be necessary, yet the rebound can be the modification of only one, since the other may continue in its path without rebound. Something more is needed in the definition of a modification, therefore, than the necessity of another concept, and to be "contained in" (a quality which is common to both properties and modes) is more than to need something else. In my opinion there is nothing in the whole created universe which does not need, for its perfect concept, the concept of everything else in the universality of things, since everything flows into every other thing is such a way that if anything is removed or changed, everything in the world will be different from what it now is. [14]

As discussed in chapter three (pp. 44–45), Leibniz here draws a distinction between a concept A's *containing* another concept, B, and A's *needing* B in order for A to be conceived. The mention of conceptual containment is a reference to Leibniz's technical notion of concept inclusion.[15] The last sentence of the passage is undoubtedly a reference to expression and Leibniz says there that every individual concept *needs*, but does not include, the concept of every other. Mates, in construing this passage, has claimed that, for Leibniz, "the concept of A needs or leads to the concept of B if and only if some part of the first expresses the second.[16] Leibniz unfortunately does little to elaborate on the relation of one concept's needing another. We can nevertheless draw from this passage the conclusion that one individual concept does not express others by containing the others in itself.

Obviously, reductionists have no difficulty satisfying this constraint. They typically believe that individual concepts only contain (non-relational) intrinsic denominations, and, so, there is no possibility of an individual concept expressing another by containing the other's concept in itself. However, the observation of the preceding paragraph may seem to present a difficulty for my earlier construal of the role of extrinsic denominations in expression. I stated that monadic expression works by means of extrinsic denominations, which have the concepts of other individuals as components, being included in individual concepts. One could then conceivably ascertain the properties of other monads by examining the extrinsic denominations of one monad.

But the passage from the de Volder correspondence clearly implies that the concepts of other individuals are not included in an individual's concept. Yet, if the concept of another individual, B, were included in an extrinsic denomination and if that extrinsic denomination were included in A's concept, then B's concept would be included in A's. The de Volder passage shows that Leibniz did not believe that A expressed B that way.

This creates no problem for my view, however. For, as was shown in chapter three, the concepts of other individuals are not included in extrinsic denominations. And so even if extrinsic denominations are included in complete individual concepts, that does not entail that the concepts of other individuals are.

In fact, not only does my view not run afoul of the de Volder passage, it aligns very well with it. It would be very much in keeping with the passage, as well as Mates's construal of it, to render expression as follows:

(25) An individual A expresses another individual B if A's concept includes an extrinsic denomination D that needs (but does not include) the concept of B.

In this rendering, D is understood to relate whatever is denominated by it to B and B is a (non-included) component[17] of D. This reckoning of monadic expression also provides an understanding of Leibniz's claim that, "all things are in a certain way contained in all things."[18] Leibniz inserts the "in a certain way" qualification because things (or, better, the concepts of things) are not actually included in other things. Yet if extrinsic denominations are included, then other things are needed, but not included, components of such denominations. This provides an account of the "certain way" in which everything is included in everything. It is this sense of expression, the one given in (25) above, that I believe Leibniz derives from NPE, and it is to that argument that I now turn.

IV. The NPE Argument for Monadic Expression

The argument from NPE to monadic expression is stated most clearly in *Primary Truths*, where Leibniz writes

> Every individual substance involves in its perfect notion the whole universe, and everything existing in it, past, present and future. For there is no thing on which some true denomination cannot be imposed from another, at all events a denomination of comparison and relation. But there is no purely extrinsic denomination. I show the same thing in many other interrelated ways.[19]

Leibniz explicitly invokes two premises for his intended result: NPE and the claim that "there is no thing on which some true denomination cannot be imposed from another, at all events a denomination of comparison and relation." The point of the latter premise can be rendered as

> (26) For every monad A and every other monad B, there is some extrinsic denomination D, such that D relates whatever is truly denominated by it to B (i.e., if R is a binary relation, then D is the property of standing in relation R to B) and D truly denominates A.

(26) tells us that every monad is related to every other in at least some respect,[20] or that, given any two things, there will always be some basis for comparing or contrasting them. Leibniz does not furnish any grounds for accepting (26), but the claim appears plausible enough on its face. And with (26) we are in a position to reconstruct the inference from (26) and my reading of NPE to expression.

NPE, when interpreted as (6), claims that there is no extrinsic denomination of a thing that is not included in the concept of that thing. Whatever extrinsic denominations that are true of a given substance A are included in A's concept. And, by (26), we know that for every other monad B there will be an extrinsic denomination that relates A to that monad and which is true of A. It follows immediately from NPE and (26) that each monad will contain extrinsic denominations in its concept that "involve" the concepts of every other monad. In other words, the conjunction of NPE and (26) directly implies that each monad expresses every other, in the sense of expression given in (25) above. For NPE, and (26), show that, as Leibniz wrote to de Volder, everything needs (but does not include) for its individual concept the concept of everything else. This reconstruction thus provides a plausible story for how expression can occur through a thing's extrinsic denominations and yet still not happen simply by a thing containing the concepts of other things in its concept.

A question arises, though, as to how one could ascertain the properties of the other individuals by examining the individual concept of A if the concepts of other individuals are not included in A's concept. Part of the very idea of monadic expression is that the sufficiently discerning mind can examine the attributes of one monad and read off all of the attributes of every other. And with the concepts of other individuals not being contained in A's concept, it is not immediately obvious how this will happen. Unfortunately, Leibniz has little to offer by way of specifics here. There is one fact to keep in mind, however. The notion of concept-inclusion is a technical one in the philosophy of Leibniz. To say that an individual concept is not included in A's concept is simply to say that the former does not satisfy, with respect to A's concept, the formal requirements for concept-inclusion. It does not necessarily mean that the former would be *inaccessible* to the sufficiently discerning mind. Suppose <father of Solomon> is included in David's concept. As has been shown, the concept <Solomon> is not included in <father of Solomon>. Yet, <Solomon> is surely a component concept of <father of Solomon>, one that is needed in order to conceive of it, and one that is combined in some way with others to form that concept. So, if God were to examine <father of Solomon>, there would be no reason to suppose that God would not see all of the components, included or not, that are combined to form the concept, as well as the precise manner in which they are combined (even if Leibniz did not have much to say about the latter[21]). In this way, God, by examining a single individual concept should be able, as a result of (26) and NPE, to read off the complete individual concepts of every other individual, despite the non-inclusion of such concepts.

Further, I see no obstacles to harmonizing this account of monadic expression with most, if not all, of the general (non-isomorphic) accounts of expression discussed earlier. For there would seem to be nothing to preclude the existence of a mapping from a monad's extrinsic denominations to the complete individual concepts of the individuals to which those denominations related that monad. For example, such a mapping could take as an input <lover of Helen> from Paris's concept and yield the individual concept of Helen as an output.[22] The mapping will likely not be one-to-one, since, for instance, Paris probably has more than one extrinsic denomination in his concept that has <Helen> as a component (such as, <lover of Helen> and <taller than Helen>). But, as discussed in section II above, it is not textually plausible to view expression as requiring the existence of a one-to-one mapping. I thus can see no reason why the view of monadic expression I have presented cannot be made to fit with Leibniz's pronouncements on expression in general.

V. The Reductionist NPE Argument for Expression

I now want to consider how one might derive monadic expression from (26) and the reductionist reading of NPE. Here, at last, we have the benefit of being able to examine an actual attempt by a reductionist interpreter to reconstruct the argument. The interpreter is none other than Robert Sleigh, and the discussion of the argument is contained in his very insightful commentary on the Leibniz-Arnauld Correspondence. I am going to employ Sleigh's treatment as the primary vehicle through which I conduct my appraisal. Though Sleigh's discussion undoubtedly has its idiosynchrocies, I believe it is, in its central contentions, highly exemplary of how a reductionist handling of the argument would have to proceed. I will do my best to indicate the places at which Sleigh and other reductionists might part company. I will also try to anticipate and address the alternative ways in which other reductionists might handle things at those points of departure. Throughout, my contention will be that the argument cannot be reconstructed in a plausible manner if NPE is read in the reductionist way.

Extrinsic Denominations and Expression 91

During the course of his analysis, Sleigh articulates a pair of important distinctions, one between weak and strong expression and the other between weak reductionist NPE and strong reductionist NPE. Sleigh defines weak expression thus:

> (27) Let x and y be individual substances in some world W; let p be some truth about y; then x weakly expresses y if and only if there is some property f such that x has f and p is derivable from the proposition that x has f.[23]

Sleigh is less formal in his characterization of strong expression. He says that each substance strongly expresses every other just in case "each substance in a world perceives every other in a sense of perception involving low-level cognition."[24] The strong thesis of expression takes notice of the many passages in which Leibniz equates a monad's expression of every other with a monad's perception of every other.[25] I will say more about the strong thesis in general and, in particular, about what Sleigh means by "low-level cognition" below. For now, I only note that, according to Sleigh, the strong thesis is likely the one Leibniz is seeking to prove in the NPE argument for expression; whereas the weak thesis is the only one whose acceptance the argument warrants.[26]

Sleigh's weak version of NPE is essentially the reductionist view of NPE with which I have been operating throughout the book. Namely, given an extrinsic denomination D of bearing relation R to a substance B, then if D is true of a substance A, then A has an intrinsic denomination F and B has an intrinsic denomination G (where F and G can be understood as single intrinsic denominations or as sets of intrinsic denominations) such that A and B's having these intrinsic denominations implies that D is true of A.[27] Sleigh's strong version of NPE can be formulated as follows:

> (28) For any substance x and any extrinsic denomination D, if D is true of x, then there is a set of intrinsic denominations F, such that x has every member of F and that x has every member of F implies that D is true of x.[28]

The principal difference between the weak and strong versions of NPE is that under the weak thesis one infers the extrinsic denomination from the denominated individual's intrinsic denominations and the intrinsic denominations of the individual to which the extrinsic denomination relates the denominated individual. But, according to the strong thesis, one can infer the extrinsic denomination from the intrinsic denominations of the denominated individual alone. Thus, by the weak view, one would infer the applicability of <taller than Socrates> to Theatetus from the respective heights of Theatetus and Socrates. But, under the strong view, one could somehow infer that <taller than Socrates> was true of Theatetus from only Theatetus's intrinsic denominations. Now, Sleigh maintains that the textual evidence more clearly supports an ascription of the weak view to Leibniz than it does the strong view.[29] And, certainly, the overwhelming majority of reductionists have adopted the weak view.[30] Unfortunately, though Sleigh's Leibniz does not accept the strong thesis, he needs that very thesis, according to Sleigh, to obtain the strong form of expression.

I will first consider Sleigh's remarks on the argument if its conclusion is interpreted as (27), the weak thesis of expression. But before this can be done, there is a preliminary matter concerning (27)'s acceptability as an account of monadic expression that must be addressed. (27) informs us that x expresses y so long as *some* (at least one) truth about y can be inferred from x's having a given property f. The word "some" is curious. Obtaining one truth about y from x's having a given property is surely not enough for monadic expression. For, according to Leibniz, that a monad x expresses the universe means that *every* fact about every other monad can be obtained from x's attributes. In the *Discourse*, Leibniz famously writes,

> Therefore, when one considers properly the connection between things, one can say that there are in the soul of Alexander, from all time, traces of all that has happened to him, and marks of everything that will happen to him—and even traces of *everything* that happens in the universe—though no one but God can know all of them.[31]

This is why Leibniz so often refers to each monad as possessing a confused omniscience. Perception of everything is contained in each soul, but the soul has distinct awareness of only a tiny portion of this infinite amount of information. As Leibniz writes in *Principles of Nature and Grace*,

> The beauty of the universe could be learnt in each soul, could one unravel all its folds which develop perceptibility only with time . . . .Each soul knows the infinite, knows everything, but confusedly.[32]

Few things are more certain in Leibniz than that the scope of the soul's expression of every other extends to *every* fact concerning the others that obtains. (27) would thus seem far too weak to count even as weak expression.[33]

Sleigh claims, however, that if a substance expressed all the others in the sense required by (27), then that substance would express "*full* information about all the created substances" in its world.[34] How can this be? Sleigh's text is not clear on this point, but a clue to what he has in mind is that he seems to envision weak expression working through the *relational* properties of substances. That is, all of the information about other substances in a world "is encoded into the relational properties of every substance in that world."[35] Perhaps the idea here is something very much like the way expression works on my view. If some extrinsic denomination involving B is true of A, then, since the complete concept of B is a component of that denomination, one could determine via that component every fact about B. In this way, so long as *some* relational fact about B can be inferred from A's having of a given property, then *any* fact about B can be inferred from it. Of course, as a reductionist, Sleigh will not permit such relational properties to be included in complete individual concepts, nor will he allow the corresponding relational accidents to inhere in individuals. When he refers to relational properties as properties, he must only mean that they are properties in the generic sense that they are true of a substance, or some such. Yet if such properties are true of a substance, the substance can express complete information about all the others in its world. I am not sure that this is what Sleigh has in mind, but it is seemingly the only way for (27) to be even a minimally plausible candidate for Leibniz's intended conclusion in the argument.

We can now consider how (27) is obtained in the argument, according to Sleigh. Sleigh states that (27) follows immediately from (26) alone.[36] This seems right. (26) states that for any monad A and any other monad B, there will be an extrinsic denomination involving B that is true of A. A's having this denomination implies a truth about B, and, in fact, it implies (if the construal of Sleigh given in the preceding paragraph is correct) every truth about B. Moreover, in light of (26), A would express every monad in its world in this manner. Again, it is important to point out that, for purposes of Sleigh's weak expression, the extrinsic denominations that (26) ensures will be true of A need not actually be *in* A or A's concept. They only need to be true of A. This is, in fact, as we shall see below, the principal difference between Sleigh's strong and weak expression. Under weak expression, the properties that express the others need not be internal to A. By contrast, under strong expression, the properties that express the others must be internal to A. As was previously mentioned, Sleigh is doubtful that (27) is Leibniz's intended result here, and I certainly agree with him. His main grounds for doubt are precisely that many of Leibniz's statements about monadic expression imply that substances express the universe through states that are internal to them. Nevertheless, (27) at least has the virtue of being a claim that follows from the premises Leibniz sets forth in the argument, which, according to Sleigh, is a trait that strong expression lacks.

Aside from not fitting many of Leibniz's descriptions of expression, there is another problem with seeing (27) as Leibniz's intended conclusion in the argument. The problem is that NPE plays no role in the argument. Sleigh explicitly states that (27) is an immediate consequence of (26) alone. What happened to NPE? Surely, any plausible account of the argument from NPE to expression must find an integral role for NPE to play in the argument. That NPE serves no purpose in obtaining (27) is simply further evidence that (27) is not an appropriate conclusion for the argument.

If Sleigh's weak version of expression does not permit a plausible rendering of the argument, then perhaps the strong version will. The strong thesis states that A expresses B just in case A perceives B in a sense of perception involving low-level cognition. Now, in order to achieve any reliable sense of the strong thesis's prospects, we must attempt to penetrate the meaning of "perception involving low-level cognition." At various points, Sleigh refers to the strong thesis as "the internal-state form of universal perception,"[37] and this provides a clue to the meaning of "low-level cognition." In this regard, Sleigh quotes Leibniz's words from the *Principles of Nature and Grace*, where Leibniz says that perception "is the inner state of the monad representing external things."[38] In order for one monad to perceive another, the first must possess an inner state that represents the second. Even clearer in this regard is this passage from the *New System*,

> And thus, since our internal sensations (those, that is to say, which are in the soul itself and not in the brain or in the subtle parts of the body) are but phenomena dependent upon external entities, or rather are really appearances ... these internal perceptions within the soul itself must arise in it from its own original constitution, that is to say through the natural representative ability (capable of expressing entities outside itself in relation to its organs).[39]

Since these perceptions are within the soul itself, they are something of which the soul has at least confused cognition. Thus, I believe that, for Sleigh, A can be said to have (at least) low-level cognition of B just in case one of A's inner states represents B.

What, by Sleigh's reckoning, can serve as an "inner state" of a monad for these purposes? Clearly, as Sleigh is a reductionist, it cannot be an extrinsic denomination. It must therefore be that a monad's intrinsic denominations are somehow what represent the external things.

And this is the point at which reductionist NPE becomes relevant in Sleigh's reconstruction. (26) reveals that an extrinsic denomination involving B is true of A. But Sleigh says that this, as just discussed, only implies weak expression. To obtain A's strong expression of B we need, according to Sleigh, a thesis asserting the reducibility of this extrinsic denomination to intrinsic denominations, as intrinsic denominations are the only aspects of a thing that can serve as inner states.[40] It would appear, then, that Leibniz's assertion of NPE is exactly what is needed here. But, as Sleigh puts it, the NPE premise is a "wolf in sheep's clothing."[41] To see why Sleigh thinks this, recall the earlier distinction between strong and weak reductionist NPE. Sleigh claims that if the strong version of NPE is what Leibniz has in mind, then the inference to strong expression goes through. According to strong NPE, the extrinsic denomination relating A to B is reducible to A's intrinsic denominations alone. That is, from the fact that A has some set of intrinsic denominations, one can infer that the extrinsic denomination relating A to B is true. And if one can infer that this denomination involving B is true of A just from A's intrinsic denominations, then we can say that a state internal to A expresses B. How else could one determine from, say, Theatetus's intrinsic denominations alone that he is taller than Socrates unless those intrinsic denominations somehow expressed information about Socrates's height and whatever else was needed to infer that <taller than Socrates> was true of Theatetus?

Yet, as noted above, Sleigh believes on textual grounds independent of this argument that it is implausible to attribute the strong reductionist thesis to Leibniz. Rather, the textual evidence supports an ascription of the weak thesis to Leibniz more strongly, says Sleigh. However, if the weak thesis of NPE is what Leibniz intends here, the argument fails to establish its conclusion. Under the weak view, the extrinsic denomination relating A to B reduces to intrinsic denominations of A *and* B. One infers that the extrinsic denomination applies to A from both A's having certain intrinsic denominations and B's having certain intrinsic denominations. But if this were the sort of reducibility at work in the argument for expression, then no internal state of A represents B. One could not derive any truth about B from A's intrinsic denominations alone. So, according to Sleigh, we only have textual grounds for imputing the weak reductionist view of NPE to Leibniz, but Leibniz needs the strong view of NPE to reach strong expression. This is why NPE is a wolf in sheep's clothing.

I hasten to add that, in addition to its textual unfoundedness, the strong reductionist version of NPE is philosophically implausible on its face. For I simply cannot see how one could determine the truth of one of A's extrinsic denominations from A's non-relational denominations alone. How could one ever determine from just the fact that Theatetus was a certain height (plus whatever other intrinsic denominations might be involved) that he was taller than Socrates? Indeed, the only way this could seemingly be done is if we had some means of ascertaining Socrates's attributes from Theatetus's. In other words, strong NPE is only plausible if each monad expresses every other via its intrinsic denominations. Strong reductionist NPE is none other than weak reductionism plus monadic expression. In fact, Parkinson attributes the strong view to Leibniz on precisely the basis that Leibniz held to the weak view and the doctrine of expression.[42] And if this is so, Leibniz obviously could not have employed strong NPE to prove expression, for he would have been engaged in blatantly circular reasoning. In addition to its textual weaknesses, then, strong NPE cannot plausibly be viewed as the version of NPE Leibniz employed in the argument.

By Sleigh's reckoning, then, Leibniz is in a fix. Leibniz appears to want to obtain the strong version of expression. If he wanted the weak form of expression, then why does he insert NPE into the argument, since weak expression follows from (26) alone? But if the strong form of expression is his intended result, his argument fails to establish it. Thus, working under the reductionist view of NPE, Sleigh concludes that Leibniz's argument from NPE to expression does not succeed.

Other reductionists, however, may not share Sleigh's assessment of the situation. In particular, some may very well assert that a monad can express others via its intrinsic denominations without the strong reductionist thesis being true. Mates, for instance, subscribes to the weak reductionist view but maintains that expression can work just fine under that view.[43] So long as there is a mapping from the intrinsic denominations of each monad to the intrinsic denominations of every other, we have, says Mates, what we need for expression. Mates even sets forth a rather clever mapping that would serve such a purpose.[44]

Now, I will simply concede that Mates's numerical model, or some other, will work for these purposes. More generally, I will concede that monadic expression is consistent with the weak reductionist view of NPE. There is still a serious problem facing the reductionist, however. In the context of Leibniz's argument from NPE to expression a mere consistency of the two doctrines is not nearly enough. The game is to show how weak reductionist NPE *implies* monadic expression. And I, along with Sleigh, do not see how the weak view can accomplish this. We have from (26) that *at least one* extrinsic denomination involving B is true of A, and we have from weak reductionist NPE that this denomination reduces to intrinsic denominations of A and B. How does this *entail* the existence of a function which can take A's intrinsic denominations as inputs and yield *all* of B's intrinsic denominations as outputs? How does this show that a mind of sufficient capacity could ascertain *all* of the properties of B from A's concept alone? Perhaps there is some subtle way that the two premises entail monadic expression, but I am presently at a loss to see what it is.

For this reason, I believe Sleigh understands something that other reductionists do not. Sleigh makes a serious attempt to reconstruct Leibniz's inference from reductionist NPE to expression and he determines, correctly, that only the strong reducibility thesis could actually imply strong expression. Yet because the strong reducibility thesis is textually, as well as philosophically, unsatisfactory, Sleigh does not impute it to Leibniz, claiming instead that Leibniz adhered to the weak reducibility thesis. The upshot of all of this for

Sleigh is that Leibniz made a bad argument. Other reductionists, working in isolation from the demands of this argument, content themselves with the claim that the weak reducibility thesis is consistent with strong expression. They claim a monad can express all the others via its intrinsic denominations by means of a computational procedure by which one could employ these intrinsic denominations to determine all of the intrinsic denominations of all the others. This claim, while perhaps true, is not sufficient. There is no clear way in which it can be made to follow from the combination of (26) and the weak reductionist interpretation of NPE. Sleigh recognizes the need to make reductionist NPE fit in the context of the argument and also recognizes that the argument does not work when NPE is taken this way.

However, instead of seeing the reductionist reading of NPE as itself the source of the problem, Sleigh charges the error to Leibniz. On the other hand, I regard the argument's failure under the reductionist view to be evidence against that view. By the same token, I consider the ease with which the argument's conclusion follows under my construal of NPE to be strong evidence for that construal. Because (26) and my reading of NPE imply that an extrinsic denomination involving B is itself included in A's concept (along with the corresponding relational accident being inherent in A), there is an *internal* state of A that expresses B. A's concept contains an extrinsic denomination that needs but does not include B's concept, and, for Leibniz, a concept that is needed but not included is one that is expressed. My reading of NPE in conjunction with (26) thus provides exactly what is needed to reach the result Leibniz sought in the argument.

Appendix

A Critique of Massimo Mugnai's Version of NPE

Massimo Mugnai's *Leibniz's Theory of Relations* is the only other book besides this one that is entirely about Leibniz's views on relations and extrinsic denominations. The interpretation Mugnai develops is, in some respects, similar to the reductionist one espoused by Mates, Cover and Hawthorne, and others. For example, he claims that, for Leibniz, the only accidents to be found in substances are intrinsic, non-relational ones.[1] Unlike most reductionists, however, he asserts that Leibniz allowed relational properties to be included in complete individual concepts.[2] Mugnai, in opposition to what has come to be called the Russell-Couturat Thesis, thus believes that, for Leibniz, what is true at the level of individual concepts is not always true at the level of substances and their accidents. Mugnai also does not appear to accept the reductionist reading of NPE:

> On several occasions Leibniz unequivocally expresses the conviction that, if a relation existing between two or more subjects changes, this implies a change in all correlated subjects. Sometimes he expresses this by asserting that "from a strict metaphysical point of view . . . there is no purely extrinsic denomination." . . . Since it seems to me that this assertion has given rise to misleading interpretations, it is essential to clarify its meaning. First of all, it must not be mistaken for the logical-ontological assertion that every extrinsic relation or denomination is founded on specific qualities in the correlated objects . . . . What Leibniz is maintaining is that there can be no mutation of a given relation without this having its effect on the intrinsic qualities of all the correlated objects.[3]

So, for Mugnai, NPE is the claim that

(M1) A change of extrinsic denomination implies a change in the denominated thing (and any other thing(s) to which the denomination relates the denominated thing).

(M1), for all intents and purposes, is just (9) from chapter two. When Mugnai states in the above passage that NPE "must not be mistaken for the logical-ontological assertion that every extrinsic relation or denomination is founded on specific qualities in the correlated objects," I believe he means to distance himself from the standard reductionist reading of NPE. (M1) is clearly not the same understanding of NPE that reductionists endorse, nor is it the one I accept. Now, all parties will, of course, agree that Leibniz accepted (M1); but is (M1) a plausible candidate for the meaning of NPE? In what follows, I hope to show that it is not.

Mugnai's reading of NPE appears to rely heavily upon those passages in which Leibniz argues for NPE on the basis of the interconnection of all things (IC). As discussed in section III of chapter four, there is a surface plausibility, in light of such passages, to identifying NPE with (M1). For instance, Leibniz says,

> *Philalethes*. However, a change of relation can occur without there having been any change in the subject: Titius, "whom I consider today as a father, ceases to be so tomorrow, only by the death of his son, without any alteration made in himself."
>
> *Theophilus*. That can very well be said if we are guided by the things of which we are aware; but in metaphysical strictness there is no wholly extrinsic denomination, because of the real connections amongst all things.[4]

It would be much too hasty, however, simply to equate NPE with (M1) on the basis of such passages. For there is a wider context to Leibniz's remarks above that makes another reading of NPE fit equally well. Leibniz is responding to Locke. Locke, as shown in section IV of chapter four essentially takes as a given that extrinsic denominations are not properties of what they denominate, and it was for that reason that he believed they could change without any alteration occurring in the denominated thing. That is, Locke was committed to

> (L) If extrinsic denominations are not properties of what they denominate, then a change of extrinsic denomination can occur without any change occurring in the denominated thing.

Yet Leibniz has a principle—the interconnection of all things—that directly implies the denial of the consequent of (L). The interconnection principle maintains that a change in one thing entails a change in every other. So, for any individual, A, if one of A's extrinsic denominations changes as a result of a change in some other individual, B, then interconnection guarantees that A will change as well. Now, the denial of the consequent of (L) just is what (M1) asserts, and thus I do not mean to deny that (M1) would be a natural claim for Leibniz to make in this setting. However, this consideration of the Lockean backdrop demonstrates that another reading of NPE is natural in this setting: the reading that reckons NPE as (6). For, on that reading, NPE is essentially the denial of the antecedent of (L). And since interconnection implies the negation of the consequent of (L), the denial of the antecedent also follows. It would thus have been just as appropriate for Leibniz to assert (6) in response to Locke as to assert (M1). Locke claims that because extrinsic denominations are not genuine properties, a change of extrinsic denomination can occur without any change in the denominated individual. Leibniz's response is that in reality, extrinsic denominations *are* genuine properties because, as dictated by the interconnection of all things, any change of extrinsic denomination is always accompanied by a change in the denominated individual. And in light of (6)'s appropriateness here, it is by no means obvious that (M1) is the understanding of NPE that Leibniz employed in passages like the above.

More significantly, though (M1) could serve as the meaning of NPE in the interconnection argument, it does not function well at all as the conclusion of Leibniz's other arguments for NPE. Consider first of all the PS argument for NPE:

> It also follows that there are no purely extrinsic denominations, which have no foundation in the thing denominated. For the notion of the subject denominated must involve the notion of the predicate; consequently, as often as the denomination of the thing is changed, there must be some variation in the thing itself.[5]

In looking at this passage, it would be rather natural to assume that NPE and the claim that, "as often as the denomination of the thing is changed, there must be some variation in the thing itself," are presented as two separate claims.[6] Nevertheless, the latter claim is (M1), Mugnai's rendering of NPE, and so, if we are to accept Mugnai's interpretation, then, despite appearances, we must accept that Leibniz is stating the same conclusion twice in the passage. In effect, Mugnai must read Leibniz as saying, "there are no purely extrinsic denominations, for the notion of the predicate must be included in the notion of the subject; consequently, there are no purely extrinsic denominations." Yet, though this is awkward, it does not by itself rule out Mugnai's view here.

A far more serious problem looms, however. There appears to be no plausible reconstruction for the PS argument if NPE is read as (M1). Now, Mugnai does not attempt to reconstruct the argument, but I believe the following closely approximates how an attempt at reconstruction would have to go under his view. PS tells us that, in true propositions, the concept of the predicate is contained in the concept of the subject. So, if a proposition truly predicates an extrinsic denomination of a subject, then that denomination will be included in the concept of the subject. Mugnai, in stark opposition to reductionists, allows for the inclusion of extrinsic denominations in complete individual concepts, and thus he likely will accept that extrinsic denominations can function as predicates of propositions, and are included in individual concepts because of PS. And if extrinsic denominations are included in individual concepts as a result of PS, then it would seem to follow that

(M2) A change of extrinsic denomination is always accompanied by a change in the concept of the denominated thing.

For if an extrinsic denomination ceases to denominate an individual, then that individual's concept will change, in that the extrinsic denomination will no longer be included in it.

(M2) is, of course, not the same claim as (M1). Many interpreters, including myself, would accept that, because of the close connection between metaphysics and logic in Leibniz, establishing (M2) is tantamount to establishing (M1).[7] Mugnai cannot do this, however. For he purports to drive a wedge between logic and metaphysics in Leibniz. Mugnai claims that while Leibniz allows extrinsic denominations to be included in complete individual concepts, he does not allow the corresponding relational accidents to inhere in individuals. We cannot simply assume, then, that if a change in an individual's concept occurs as a result of a change in one of her extrinsic denominations, there will also be a change in her. It would seem therefore that at least one additional premise is needed in order to obtain (M1).

A claim that, together with (M2), would yield (M1) directly is

(M3) A change in the concept of an individual implies a change in the individual falling under that concept.

It is clear from Mugnai's discussion that he would accept (M3), for he explicitly attributes the following closely related claim to Leibniz:

(M4) If any proposition whose subject concept is the concept of an individual changes from true to false (and vice versa), then there must be a change in the individual who falls under that concept.[8]

Indeed, given Leibniz's conceptual containment theory of truth (i.e., PS), (M3) and (M4) are materially equivalent. For, it is a corollary of the conceptual containment theory, that

(M5) A proposition whose subject concept is the concept of an individual changes from true to false if and only if there is a change in the concept of that individual.

(M5) and (M3) imply (M4); and, similarly, (M5) and (M4) imply (M3).

In fact, since Mugnai explicitly attributes (M4) to Leibniz and since (M3) follows from (M4) and (M5), we can regard (M4) as the claim that Mugnai would employ to obtain (M3), and (M3) would then be used to bridge the gap between (M2) and (M1). This, I believe, is along the general lines of how Mugnai would have to reconstruct the argument from PS to his version of NPE.

The key move in the foregoing reconstruction was the insertion of (M4) into the argument. (M4) is what ultimately allows one to infer that changes in the concept of an individual are always accompanied by changes in that individual. But (M4) cannot justifiably be inserted in this way just because it is expedient to do so. There must be good grounds in the text of Leibniz for attributing (M4) to Leibniz, and also good grounds for thinking (M4) is a claim Leibniz was implicitly relying on in this setting. With regard to the former, Mugnai states that Leibniz's acceptance of (M4) is based on the interconnection of all things.[9] (M4) would be unproblematic in cases where a proposition concerning a given subject changes from true to false when that proposition predicates an *intrinsic* denomination of that subject. There would clearly be a change in the subject that corresponded to the change in the truth value of the relevant proposition. And there would also be no problem in a case where one of the subject's extrinsic denominations ceases to denominate the subject as a result of a change in one of the subject's own intrinsic denominations. But what about a case in which a proposition ascribing an extrinsic denomination to that subject changes from true to false as a result of a change in another individual's intrinsic denominations? In this case, we would need to know that interconnection was true (i.e., that a change in one thing entails a change in every other) to be assured that (M4) was true. Hence, according to Mugnai, the interconnection doctrine is Leibniz's justification for accepting (M4).

But this creates a serious problem with regard to the latter of the above conditions, the condition that there must be good grounds for thinking (M4) is a claim that Leibniz is implicitly relying upon in the argument. The problem is that interconnection, as shown in section III of chapter four, directly implies (M1) and this means that PS is superfluous to showing (M1). Since Mugnai's reconstruction must use (M4) to obtain (M1) and since (M4) is derived from interconnection, then Mugnai's reconstruction must ultimately employ interconnection as a premise. Yet interconnection *by itself* implies (M1). Are we to believe that in arguing from PS to NPE, Leibniz employs an *unstated* premise that renders PS extraneous to the argument? Such a view is simply not a plausible reckoning of what Leibniz had in mind in the argument.

I have much less to say about how Mugnai's view of NPE fares with respect to the other two arguments. The reason for this is that I have simply not been able to arrive at even a rough general sense of how the arguments might proceed under his view. With regard to the IC and PS arguments for NPE, it was fairly clear how an argument to his view of NPE would run. But with regard to the Identity of Indiscernibles (ID) and Expression arguments, no even semi-natural or semi-plausible approach has occurred to me. In the ID argument, Leibniz says, "there are no purely extrinsic denominations, because . . . it is not possible for two things to differ from one another is respect of place and time alone, but that it is always necessary that there shall be some other internal difference."[10] To see this argument as leading to Mugnai's NPE we have to see how the fact that

> (P) Two distinct things cannot differ in terms of place alone; there must be a genuine accident which one has and the other lacks.

implies that

> (M1) A change of extrinsic denomination implies a change in the denominated thing.

As discussed in section V of chapter five, if two things differ in place, then they will have differing relations of situation to other fixed coexistents. Presumably, Mugnai would regard a showing that

> (M6) As often as a thing's relations of situation change, there will be a change in that thing

as tantamount to showing his version of NPE.[11] But how can we obtain (M6) from (P)? Specifically, how does the notion of a *change* in a relation of situation even enter into the argument, since (P) has nothing to say about any sort of change? (P) by itself just does not appear to carry any straightforward implications about whether a thing changes when its relations of situation change. There could be some way to supplement (P) with another claim or claims to obtain Mugnai's view of NPE. I have no idea what the additional claim(s) would be though. It certainly could not be the interconnection principle, since that principle alone establishes Mugnai's NPE and would thus render (P) irrelevant to the argument. Beyond interconnection, no other candidates come to mind.

Matters are equally puzzling if we try to envision how monadic expression might follow from Mugnai's NPE. Recall that Leibniz offers two premises in his argument from NPE to expression: NPE and

> (26) For every monad A and every other monad B, there is some extrinsic denomination D, such that D relates whatever is truly denominated

by it to B (i.e., if R is a binary relation, then D is the property of standing in relation R to B) and D truly denominates A.

(26) ensures that at least one extrinsic denomination involving B will be true of A. Mugnai's version of NPE then informs us that as often as *this* denomination (and any other) changes, there will be a change in A. Now, how do these two claims demonstrate, or even suggest, that from the properties of A alone one could infer *all* of the properties of B? A natural way of closing the gap does not suggest itself here, and thus anything I offer on behalf of Mugnai would be sheer speculation. Perhaps there is some reasonable way of arriving at expression from Mugnai's view of NPE, but my suspicion is that in this argument, as well as in the others, his NPE is just not what Leibniz had in mind.

References

Adams, Robert. *Leibniz: Determinist, Theist, Idealist*. Oxford: Oxford University Press, 1994.
Bennett, Jonathan. *Locke, Berkeley, Hume: Central Themes*. Oxford: Clarendon Press, 1971.
Broad, C. D. *Leibniz: An Introduction*. Cambridge: Cambridge University Press, 1975.
Brown, Gregory. "Compossibility, Harmony and Perfection in Leibniz." *The Philosophical Review* 96 (1987): 173–203.
Burdick, Howard. "What Was Leibniz's Problem About Relations?" *Synthese* 88 (1991): 1–13.
Cover, J. A. and John O'Leary-Hawthorne. *Substance and Individuation in Leibniz*. London: Cambridge University Press, 1999.
D'Agostino, Fred. "Leibniz on Compossibility and Relational Predicates." *Philosophical Quarterly* 26 (1976): 125–38. Reprinted in *Leibniz: Metaphysics and Philosophy of Science*, edited by R. S. Woolhouse. Oxford: Oxford University Press, 1981.
Gibson, James. *Locke's Theory of Knowledge and Its Historical Relations*. Cambridge: Cambridge University Press, 1960.
Hintikka, Jaakko. "Leibniz on Plenitude, Relations and the 'Reign of Law'," in *Leibniz: A Collection of Critical Essays*, edited by Harry Frankfurt. New York: Anchor Books, 1972.
Ishiguro, Hide. "Leibniz's Theory of the Ideality of Relations," in *Leibniz: A Collection of Critical Essays*, edited by Harry Frankfurt. New York: Anchor Books, 1972.
—. *Leibniz's Philosophy of Logic and Language*. 2nd ed. Cambridge: Cambridge University Press, 1990.
Kulstad, Mark. "A Closer Look At Leibniz's Alleged Reduction of Relations." *Southern Journal of Philosophy* 18 (1980): 417–32.
—. "Leibniz's Conception of Expression." *Studia Leibnitiana* 9 (1977): 55–76.
Langton, Rae. "Locke's Relations and God's Good Pleasure." *Proceedings of the Aristotelian Society* 100 (2000): 75–91.
Leibniz, Gottfried Wilhelm. *Die Philosophichen Schriften*. Edited by C. I. Gerhardt. 7 vols. Berlin: Weidmannsche Buchhandlung, 1857–1890.
—. *Die Leibniz-Handschriften der Koniglichen offentlichen Bibliothek zu Hanover*. Edited by E. Bodemann. Hanover: 1895; Reprinted Hildesheim, 1966.
—. *De Summa Rerum: Metaphysical Papers, 1676–1676*. Translated and edited by G. H. R. Parkinson. New Haven: Yale University Press, 1992.
—. *Leibniz: Logical Papers*. Translated and edited by G. H. R. Parkinson. Oxford: Oxford University Press, 1966.
—. *Leibniz: Philosophical Papers and Letters*. Translated and edited by L. E. Loemker. 2nd ed. Dordrecht: D. Reidel, 1969.

―. *Leibniz: Philosophical Writings*. Translated by Mary Morris and G. H. R. Parkinson. Edited by G. H. R. Parkinson. London: J. M. Dent, 1973.

―. *New Essays on Human Understanding*. Translated and edited by Peter Remnant and Jonathan Bennett. Cambridge: Cambridge University Press, 1996.

―. *Textes inedits d'apres de la bibliotheque provinicale de Hanovre*. Edited by G. Grua. 2 vols. Paris: [PUB], 1948.

Locke, John. *An Essay Concerning Human Understanding*. Edited by Peter H. Nidditch. Oxford: Oxford University Press, 1975.

Mates, Benson. *The Philosophy of Leibniz: Metaphysics and Language*. New York: Oxford University Press, 1986.

McCullough, Lawrence. *Leibniz on Individuals and Individuation: The Persistence of Premodern Ideas in Modern Philosophy*. Dodrecht: Kluwer Academic Publishers, 1996.

McRae, Robert. *Leibniz: Perception, Apperception, and Thought*. Toronto: University of Toronto Press, 1976.

Mugnai, Massimo. *Leibniz' Theory of Relations*. Stuttgart: Franz Steiner Verlag, 1992.

Parkinson, G. H. R. *Logic and Reality in Leibniz's Metaphysics*. Oxford: Oxford University Press, 1965.

Rescher, Nicholas. "Leibniz's Interpretation of His Logical Calculi." *The Journal of Symbolic Logic* 19 (1954): 1–13.

―. *The Philosophy of Leibniz*. Englewood Cliffs, NJ: Prentice Hall, 1967.

Russell, Bertrand. *A Critical Exposition of the Philosophy of Leibniz*. 2nd ed. London: George Allen and Unwin, 1937.

―. *My Philosophical Development*. New York: Simon and Schuster, 1959.

Sleigh, Robert C. *Leibniz and Arnauld: A Commentary on Their Correspondence*. New Haven: Yale University Press, 1990.

―. "Truth and Sufficient Reason in the Philosophy of Leibniz," in *Leibniz: Critical and Interpretive Essays*, edited by Michael Hooker. Minneapolis: University of Minnesota Press, 1982.

Swoyer, Chris. "Leibniz's Calculus of Real Addition." *Studia Leibnitiana* 26 (1994): 1–30.

―. "Leibniz on Intension and Extension." *Nous* 29 (1995): 96–114.

―. "Leibnizian Expression." *Journal of the History of Philosophy* 33 (1995): 65–99.

Woolhouse, R. S. *Locke*. Minneapolis: University of Minnesota Press, 1983.

Abbreviations

The following abbreviations have been used in citing the works of Leibniz:

DSR: Leibniz, Gottfried Wilhelm. *De Summa Rerum: Metaphysical Papers, 1676–1676.* Translated and edited by G. H. R. Parkinson. New Haven: Yale University Press, 1992.

G: ——. *Die Philosophichen Schriften.* Edited by C. I. Gerhardt. 7 vols. Berlin: Weidmannsche Buchhandlung, 1857–1890.

Grua: ——. *Textes inedits d'apres de la bibliotheque provinicale de Hanovre.* Edited by G. Grua. 2 vols. Paris: 1948.

L: ——. *Leibniz: Philosophical Papers and Letters.* Translated and edited by L. E. Loemker. 2nd ed. Dordrecht: D. Reidel, 1969.

LH: ——. *Die Leibniz-Handschriften der Koniglichen offentlichen Bibliothek zu Hanover.* Edited by E. Bodemann. Hanover: 1895; Reprinted Hildesheim, 1966.

LLP: ——. *Leibniz: Logical Papers.* Translated and edited by G. H. R. Parkinson. Oxford: Oxford University Press, 1966.

NE: ——. *New Essays on Human Understanding.* Translated and edited by Peter Remnant and Jonathan Bennett. Cambridge: Cambridge University Press, 1996.

PW: ——. *Leibniz: Philosophical Writings.* Translated by Mary Morris and G. H. R. Parkinson. Edited by G. H. R. Parkinson. London: J. M. Dent, 1973.

Notes

Introduction

1. PW, 133.
2. One of the best general discussions to this effect is found in Kulstad (1980).
3. An example of a non-reductionist account that is, I believe, less than satisfactory is that given by Ishiguro. See Ishiguro (1972), 193 and (1990), 134. For a brief presentation and evaluation of her view see note 34 of chapter one.
4. PW, 89 (L, 268) and L, 365.
5. See e.g., NE, 227.
6. See e.g., PW, 133
7. My discussion is confined to NPE's place in Leibniz's metaphysics. I do not take up the implications a proper understanding of NPE could hold for Leibniz's practical philosophy. I leave that for another time.

Chapter One

1. Mates acknowledges that the notion of reference via a quantified variable is less than entirely clear (See Mates, 219, n.33), and he does not offer any examples of this sort of reference. A possible example of such a denomination is the denomination expressed by the description, "a father." That an individual, A, has this denomination means there is some other individual that A is the father of. The denomination would apparently make reference to this individual and would do so by means of a quantified variable.
2. Mates, 218.
3. Ibid., 219.
4. I will use the "<...>" notation throughout the book to indicate when I am speaking of a denomination or other type of concept.
5. Mates, 219.
6. According to Leibniz, every individual substance has a complete individual concept—a concept that contains every property that can be truly attributed to that substance, and under which that and only that substance falls. In a characteristic passage, he states: "In the perfect concept of each individual substance is contained all its predicates, both necessary and contingent, past, present, and future." G VII, 311.
7. Some interpreters have maintained that in order for an alleged reduction to really count as a reduction the resulting set of propositions must be logically equivalent to the original proposition. See e.g., Russell (1959), 55. And yet since, in the case of asymmetric relations, one apparently cannot reach an equivalent set without at least one proposition involving a relation, Leibniz's alleged reductionist claim is judged implausible. Mates disagrees with these commentators' insistence upon logical equiva-

lence, claiming instead that arriving at a set from which the proposition containing the extrinsic denomination can be inferred is enough to claim that the proposition has been reduced, and that this is the only sort of reduction Leibniz had in mind. Mates, 216–18. This debate may be of some interest as concerning the nature of reductions in general, but it will be futile as a debate concerning the text of Leibniz, if, as I claim, Leibniz was not a reductionist in the first place.

8. My discussion in this section is very much indebted to Kulstad's. See Kulstad (1980).

9. Russell (1937), 12–14.

10. Leibniz's view of truth will be discussed in much greater detail in chapter two.

11. LLP, 13.

12. Mates implies that such passages provide evidence for reductionism. See Mates, 214, 216.

13. Ibid.

14. I suspect the idea is that if we are given that Peter is similar to Paul and that that can be analyzed into "Peter is now A" and "Paul is now A," then we may legitimately infer that Paul is similar to Peter, since the analysis of the premise ("Peter is now A" and "Paul is now A"), along with the commutativity of conjunction, is also the analysis of the conclusion.

15. Mates, 14–15. Also, in a letter of 1679, Leibniz says that the reason he performs these analyses is "to make all reasonings reducible to a certain and indubitable form." Quoted in Parkinson (1965), 51.

16. LLP, 14.

17. L, 704 (PW, 232–33).

18. Ibid.

19. Ibid.

20. Kulstad (1980), 423.

21. Ibid., 424. See also Burdick (1991), McCullough (1996), 172–77, among others.

22. Kulstad (1980), 424.

23. LLP, 135.

24. Cover and Hawthorne, 73. Apparently, their point is that Solomon becomes an accident with a leg in David and a full-nelson hug around himself. See also Mates, 61–62 (though he does not offer the point as an objection to regarding extrinsic denominations as properties).

25. L, 307 (PW, 18).

26. L, 457 (PW, 122).

27. Cover and Hawthorne, 75–76. Unfortunately, Ishiguro, who believes that Leibniz did allow relational accidents, believes, as a result of his also being committed to the world-apart doctrine, that Leibniz was guilty of inconsistency. Ishiguro, 1990, 114ff. Her charge of inconsistency has provided grist for the reductionist mill ever since. Cover and Hawthorne, for example, make good use of her allegation by stating of it that, "one person's *reductio* is another person's *modus tollens*" (75–76). That is, she believes that because Leibniz held both views, he was trapped in an inconsistency; reductionists, on the other hand, see the world-apart claim as evidence against the view that he allowed relational accidents.

28. L, 269 (PW, 90), 457 (PW, 122), 611; PW, 79.
29. D'Agostino, 99.
30. L, 526–27.
31. PW, 133–34.
32. L, 609 (emphasis added).

33. Today, we would likely assume the common relation was the "father of" relation, but I am not at all certain that Leibniz understood the common relation that way. In any event, the matter does not seem crucial here.

34. Ishiguro has offered an alternative, non-reductionist account, but one that I find less than adequate. She claims that NPE should be understood as

> distinguishing extrinsic and intrinsic denominations, and saying that one cannot have the former kind of denomination without involving the latter kind....If I say, for example, that there are no purely Doric temples, I am implying that every temple that has Doric features has some features that are not Doric, but something else, e.g., Corinthian. (Ishiguro [1990], 134)

Elsewhere, she states her understanding of NPE as, "there can be no way of identifying things by extrinsic relational properties which do not involve some intrinsic property of the thing" (Ishiguro [1972], 193). I must admit that I find these formulations somewhat puzzling. The Doric temple example suggests that NPE requires extrinsic denominations to be viewed as having both extrinsic components and intrinsic components. For example, the extrinsic denomination "father" could be regarded as having the intrinsic denomination "male" as a component. Or perhaps what she means is that for any extrinsic denomination to be true of a thing, certain intrinsic denominations must be true of it as well. The required intrinsic denominations are not components of the extrinsic denomination, but are rather presupposed by it. For the extrinsic denomination "taller than Socrates" to be true of Theatetus, Theatetus must have a height that is greater than that of Socrates; Theatetus's height is an intrinsic denomination of him, but it is probably not a component of the extrinsic denomination "taller than Socrates." Both of these readings of Ishiguro's interpretation of NPE display some degree of fit with her remarks. Perhaps neither reading is what she has in mind. In any case, aside from the fairly overt ambiguity of her remarks, the principal shortcoming of her interpretation is that she does not demonstrate how her reading of NPE fits into the context of Leibniz's arguments for NPE. I do not believe either of the readings I propose of her interpretation are plausible candidates for the conclusion of Leibniz's arguments for NPE, nor do they make very likely candidates as premises for the doctrine of expression.

35. There are other interpreters who seem to hold something close to this understanding of NPE. Hintikka, for example, writes that NPE "can be understood not as denying the reality or the irreducibility of relational concepts, but rather as asserting their indispensability for characterizing individuals (individual substances)" (Hintikka [1972], 165). He does not develop his interpretation of NPE beyond this, however, and it is not at all certain that his above statement can be construed as another way of stating (6). Kulstad also seems to hold something close to my view. He argues, as I also

do in chapter two, that, as a consequence of Leibniz's predicate-in-subject doctrine of truth, every denomination, even relational ones, is included in the concept of the denominated individual (Kulstad [1980], 427). He does not, however, explicitly offer this as an interpretation of NPE, and, based on certain aspects of his discussion, I am not certain that he would.

36. For a description of Leibniz's doctrine of complete individual concepts see note 12 above.

37. Leibniz's also distinguishes between properties and accidents. Properties are essentially concepts of accidents; accidents are what are in the individual and properties are what are in the concept of the individual. And there is an extremely tight parallel between the accidents that are in the individual and the properties that are in the individual's concept. It seems even fair to say that A is an accident of a given individual just in case the concept of A is included in that individual's concept. Not all interpreters agree with this reading of Leibniz, though. See, for example, Mugnai, 117, 121–22.

38. NE, 401 (emphasis added). See also L, 500, where Leibniz says, "For I ask whether this volition or command, or if you prefer, this divine law once established, has bestowed upon things only an extrinsic denomination or whether it has truly conferred upon them some created impression which endures within them."

Chapter Two

1. Among numerous passages that could be cited, the following are exemplary: "A true proposition is one whose predicate is contained in its subject" (*The Nature of Truth*, in PW, 93). "[I]n every affirmative true proposition, necessary or contingent universal or singular, the notion of the predicate is contained in some way in that of the subject...or else I do not know what truth is" (*Correspondence with Arnauld*, PW, 62).

2. *Discourse on Metaphysics*, sec. 8, in PW, 18.

3. PW, 89 (L, 268). In another passage, Leibniz says, "there are no extrinsic denominations and no one becomes a widower in India by the death of his wife in Europe unless a real change occurs in him. For every predicate is in fact contained in the nature of the subject" (L, 365).

4. Given the way Leibniz presents the argument, it is also possible to construe the sequence as beginning with PS, then inferring from PS that as often as the denomination of a thing is changed, there is a change in the thing itself, and then inferring NPE from that. The issue of whether we should construe the argument this way and of how the reconstruction of it would look if we did is discussed in note 46 of chapter two below.

5. PW, 87–88 (L, 267–68).

6. See e.g., Russell (1937), 12–14 and Rescher (1967), 72–73.

7. See Mates, 220, Rescher (1967), 72–73 and Cover and Hawthorne, 69–70.

8. Russell advanced a very similar argument to this for the conclusion that Leibniz held to the reducibility of relations and relational properties. Russell (1937), 12–14. Russell's argument, instead of beginning with the PS principle, begins with Leibniz's

alleged belief that every proposition has a subject and a predicate (or, as some interpreters put it, that every proposition is in subject-predicate form). From there, the argument asserts that propositions containing extrinsic denominations are not in subject-predicate form, because extrinsic denominations are not predicate concepts; only intrinsic denominations can serve as predicate concepts. Hence, any proposition containing an extrinsic denomination must reduce to a set of propositions all of whose members are in subject-predicate form (i.e., a set in which each member has an intrinsic denomination as its predicate concept). Now, Russell, upon claiming that Leibniz believed every proposition had a subject and a predicate and that extrinsic denominations were not predicate concepts, might well have concluded that, for Leibniz, propositions containing extrinsic denominations were not propositions at all. But Russell, likely finding the denial of propositional status counterintuitive, not to mention implausible as an interpretation of Leibniz, claims that Leibniz was committed to the reducibility of such propositions.

9. G, VII, 311.
10. PW, 57.
11. L, 310.
12. Ibid., 307–8. For a more comprehensive treatment of these and other textual considerations relevant to this point see Kulstad, 419–23.
13. Cover and Hawthorne, 64.
14. In this vein, Cover and Hawthorne say: "a commitment to irreducibly relational facts about individual substances does not follow from the use of relational predicates. Why should it? Unless one thinks that how we speak gives really reliable insight into the deep nature of what there is"(69).
15. They actually cite these two passages to support a slightly different point. They claim that the passages display a "reductive tone," and that they support the claim that complete individual concepts do not contain extrinsic denominations, but only the intrinsic denominations that serve as a foundation for them—i.e., from which the extrinsic denominations can be inferred (Cover and Hawthorne, 70). They do not explicitly state that the passages provide grounds for the sort of restriction on PS's applicability I speak of in the text above. However, I believe it is fair to extend their use of the passages to this. For Leibniz derives his doctrine of complete individual concepts from the PS principle. See e.g., PW, 57. The concepts that are included in complete individual concepts are so included because of the PS principle. Thus, if complete individual concepts contain only intrinsic denominations as Cover and Hawthorne maintain, then it seems they should also maintain that PS can only apply to propositions having intrinsic denominations as predicate concepts.
16. Cover and Hawthorne, 70. (their emphasis). The quote from the *Discourse on Metaphysics* can be found at PW, 19 (L, 308).
17. PW, 57–58.
18. See chapter one, pp. 9–11.
19. PW, 62 (L, 337).
20. Broad (1975), 11. Robert Sleigh concurs at (1982), 213.
21. PW, 93.

22. From *Metaphysical Consequences of the Principle of Reason*, sec. 1, in PW, 172.
23. PW, 87 (L, 267).
24. PW, 172.
25. PW, 87 (L, 267).
26. Leibniz's views on necessary and contingent propositions impose the need to qualify his claim that every true proposition has an a priori proof. Necessary propositions, at least in principle, can be shown identical by means of an a priori proof that is finite in length. Showing contingent propositions identical, however, requires an *a priori* analysis that is infinitely long. The analysis never reaches an end. This does not mean that the predicate is not in the subject or that such propositions are not identical, or that they lack a reason; it only means that these things cannot be shown so by a completable *a priori* proof. In *On Freedom*, Leibniz says,

> in the case of contingent truths, even though the predicate is in the subject, this can never be demonstrated of it, nor can the proposition ever be reduced to an equation or identity. Instead, the analysis proceeds to infinity, God alone seeing—not, indeed, the end of the analysis, since it has no end—but the connection of the terms or the inclusion of the predicate in the subject, for he sees whatever is in the series. (PW, 109)

27. PW, 172.
28. PW, 87–88 (L, 267–68). See also PW, 93–94 and 172, among others.
29. PW, 7–8. And in *Of Universal Synthesis and Analysis*, he says, "And so a reason can be given for each truth; for the connection of the predicate with the subject is either self-evident, as in the case of identities, or it has to be displayed, which is done by the analysis of the terms" (PW, 15).
30. Mates also takes this reading of the passage. Mates, 63. See also, Adams, 65.
31. PW, 7, 8.
32. See section IV of chapter three for a discussion of another way of forming complex concepts that Leibniz appears to have accepted.
33. PW, 12. I present a more detailed discussion of Leibniz's views on how complex concepts are formed out of simpler ones in chapter three.
34. From *A Specimen of Discoveries About Marvellous Secrets of Nature in General*, in PW, 75. See also PW, 15, 18, 87–88, 93–94, 172, among others.
35. Of course, for Leibniz, if such a proposition were contingent, then, though it would still be identical, it could not be shown to be identical by any finitely long a priori proof. See note 26 of chapter two above.
36. Strictly speaking, carrying an analysis of a complex concept through to the level of simple concepts is, according to Leibniz, beyond human abilities (PW, 8). Thus, we cannot come to see that a proposition is identical by analyzing the predicate into its primitive concepts and then determining that those primitive concepts are also included in the subject. Leibniz believes that all true propositions are identical, but he also thinks that there are only a relatively small number of them whose identicalness we can demonstrate (PW, 15). But, again, the fact that we cannot prove a proposition identical via an *a priori* proof does not count against its being identical.

Presumably, for those propositions whose identicalness we can show, we do so by means of analyzing their subject and predicate concepts *simultaneously* and just far enough to reach an identity. We would not necessarily need to carry the analysis to the level of primitive concepts for the identity to become apparent (PW, 94).

37. Though, as I argue in chapter three, section IV, extrinsic denominations cannot be formed by putting simpler concepts together in a straightforward conjunction-like manner.

38. Although the *composite* of such primitive concepts is, according to my view, included in Alexander's concept, this does not mean that *each* of those primitive concepts is individually included in his concept. This matter, along with its implications for the conceptual structure of extrinsic denominations, is taken up in sections III and IV of chapter three.

39. PW, 87–88 (L, 267–68).
40. PW, 89 (L, 268).
41. Ibid., 62 (L, 337).
42. Ibid., 78, 90, among other passages. I argue in section II of chapter four that this is how Leibniz's doctrine of the interconnection of all things should be interpreted.
43. L, 308 (PW, 19), L, 269 (PW, 90). How it is, according to Leibniz, that the properties of a monad communicate this immense quantity of information has been the subject of much scholarly discussion and debate, but it is enough for the moment that a single monad's properties can communicate such information. I discuss the question of how monads express the universe in chapter six.
44. It is not entirely certain that the expression doctrine would genuinely imply this change in Bernard's properties. It may be that Bernard's properties can express Andrew's new height without any alteration occurring in them. Whether such a change in Bernard's properties is or is not implied by (13) would, I suppose, depend on the precise way in which monads express the properties of other monads. Obviously, if expression does not mandate such a change, then that is simply further reason to reject (13) as a way to arrive at (9) from NPE.
45. The argument reads: "Every individual substance involves in its perfect notion the whole universe, and everything existing in it, past, present and future. For there is no thing on which some true denomination cannot be imposed from another, at all events a denomination of comparison and relation. But there is no purely extrinsic denomination" (PW, 90). For the argument for (12), also see PW, 90.
46. L, 365. Also quoted in note 3 of chapter two above.
47. As noted earlier, there is an issue as to whether Leibniz's claims in the PS argument should be ordered in the sequence that I have presented them. It is possible, given the way he formulates the argument, that Leibniz intended the argument to move directly from (7) to (9) and then from (9) to NPE. I think that in terms of the wording and structure of the passage this alternative sequence is less plausible than the one I have opted for. Moreover, it is rather difficult to envision how a reconstruction of the alternative sequence would go, which is also an indication that the original sequence is preferable. Under my interpretation of NPE, the argument seemingly must arrive at NPE before it can arrive at (9). For, to my mind, PS implies (9) because PS implies that any denomination (intrinsic or extrinsic) that is true of a thing is in-

cluded in the concept of that thing. Recall Leibniz's remark from *Primary Truths* that PS is the basis of truth in the case of both an intrinsic and an extrinsic denomination. So, since, by PS, all true denominations of a thing are included in the concept of that thing, then as often as one of those denominations changes, there will be a change in that thing. Thus it first needs to be shown that extrinsic denominations are included in the concepts of what they denominate, which is what my version of NPE maintains, before we can get to (9). I cannot see any natural way of deriving (9) from PS and then inferring my version of NPE from (9). It seems that it must go the other way around. As for the reductionist interpretation, I have found it rather difficult to see how a reconstruction would go under the alternative sequence. Perhaps they could attempt to obtain (12) or (13) from PS somehow and then obtain (9) from that in the manner described in the text above, but that would be subject to the same difficulty explained above (it is implausible to suppose that Leibniz implicitly employed (12) or (13) to reach (9) only to prove them explicitly later in the essay). Further, even if the reductionist can find some way to get to (9) from PS, it is not at all clear how she will then obtain her version of NPE from (9). I cannot see even a semi-natural way of rendering the alternative sequence from the reductionist standpoint, and because of that, I fear that any reconstruction I offer on their behalf would be too speculative to be helpful. I leave the task to those who espouse that interpretation and who believe the alternative sequence is correct.

Chapter Three

1. Cover and Hawthorne, 73.

2. Perhaps their point is not that admitting relational accidents would go against the individual accident doctrine *per se*, but that it would transgress the spirit of that doctrine in some way. They do not hold the mistaken belief that "father of Solomon" would be an accident of more than one substance. They are simply claiming that if Leibniz disallows accidents to be in more than one substance, he surely would not allow an accident to be in one substance and have another substance as a constituent. Such a claim would be difficult to evaluate, though. An adherence to the former doctrine does not logically commit one to the latter. Leibniz thus could have held the former view without accepting the latter. More importantly, though, this objection still relies on the highly questionable claim that individuals are constituents of relational accidents, and so fares no better than those that I discuss in the text above.

3. LLP, 135.

4. See Leibniz's proposition 7 in LLP, 133.

5. Others have asserted such a consequence. See Mates, 63 and Brown, 191–92, n.56. Mates, however, does not offer it as a criticism of views that allow extrinsic denominations in individual concepts. Brown allows relational predicates in individual concepts, but, because of the above problem, believes we must impose some sort of restriction (the nature of which is unclear to me) upon relational predicates so that one individual concept is not included in other individual concepts.

6. *Discourse on Metaphysics*, section 8, in L, 307 (PW, 18).

7. PW, 2.

8. Leibniz made various attempts to formulate a formal logic for concepts, the best of which is probably his "A Study in the Calculus of Real Addition," in LLP, 131–44. An outstanding exposition of this work is presented in Swoyer (1994).

9. I discuss another method at the end of section IV of chapter three below.

10. See his axioms 1 and 2 in the Calculus of Real Addition.

11. See e.g., Rescher (1954), 11 and Swoyer (1994), 8, 17.

12. Mates, 60 construing Grua, 535.

13. LLP, 132.

14. The "≤" notation is due to Swoyer (1994), 9.

15. See propositions 13 and 14 in LLP, 135.

16. LLP, 20–21. See also Swoyer (1995a), 102–3.

17. Swoyer (1995a), 103.

18. Leibniz seems also to have been committed to the far less plausible converse of this assertion. See Swoyer (1995a), 103–4.

19. The relation of one concept being a component of another is obviously understood here to be more general than the relation of concept-inclusion. It encompasses concept-inclusion; that is, for any concept C and any concept A such that $A \leq C$, A is a component of C. But it also encompasses concepts which, though not included in C, are, in some sense, needed to conceive of C. This issue is discussed further in section IV.

20. See, e.g., Cover and Hawthorne, 64.

21. LLP, 132.

22. I will not here attempt a general description of the class of intrinsic denominations that fail to be expressible as real sums. I will say, though, that, as the listed examples suggest, the problem appears to be particularly severe in cases like the foregoing where one concept qualifies the concept of a *part* of a thing but does not qualify the whole thing. The concept <blue>, for instance, qualifies <eyed> but is not meant to qualify the rest of the thing. Leibniz's logic of concepts has no way of restricting the scope of the application of <blue> to <eyed> only. <Blue> thus winds up ranging over, so to speak, the entire complex concept. And when we take the extension of the complex concept, we end up picking out all the blue things which have eyes and are men; we do not arrive at just the set of blue-eyed men, which was the basis of how it was proven that <a blue-eyed man> is not a real sum.

23. L, 524.

24. LLP, 47–87.

25. Ibid., 49. Adams also appears to interpret this as a way of forming complex concepts other than real addition (Adams, 65).

26. LLP, 48.

Chapter Four

1. NE, 227. Leibniz, through the mouth of Theophilus, is here countering the view of Locke, as expressed by the words of Philalethes, found at Book II, chapter 25, section 5 of Locke's *Essay*.

2. Mates, for example, appears to equate IC with the claim that each monad expresses every other (Mates, 38). But this is clearly mistaken, or at the very least, a

careless way of speaking, as Leibniz uniformly presents expression as a *consequence* of IC rather than IC itself (PW, 72, 176, 196).

3. See note 42 of chapter two.
4. PW, 196.
5. See *Monadology*, section 61 (PW, 188–89), where Leibniz says,

> For as the whole is a plenum, which means that the whole of matter is connected, and as in a plenum every movement has some effect on distant bodies in proportion to their distance, so that each body not only is sensitive to whatever happens to them, but also by means of them is sensitive to those which touch the first bodies by which it is itself directly touched; it follows that this communication stretches out indefinitely. Consequently every body is sensitive to everything which is happening in the universe.

6. L, 96.
7. Some of Leibniz's reasons for believing this rather surprising claim are explained in the following passage from an early letter to Jacob Thomasius:

> It now remains for us to come to change. Changes are commonly and rightly classed as generation, corruption, increase, decrease, alteration and change of place or motion. Modern thinkers believe that these can all be explained by local motion alone. In the first place, the matter is obvious in the case of increase and decrease, for change of quantity occurs in a whole when a part changes its place and is either added or taken away. We need only to explain generation, corruption, and alteration through motion. I observe in advance that numerically the same change may be the generation of one being and the alteration of another; for example, since we know that putrefaction consists in little worms invisible to the naked eye, any putrid infection is an alteration of man, a generation of the worm. Hooke shows similarly in his *Micrographia* that iron rust is a minute forest which has sprung up; to rust is therefore an alteration of iron but a generation of little bushes. Moreover, generation and corruption, as well as alteration, can be explained by a subtle motion of parts. For example, since white is what reflects the most light and black is what reflects the least, those things whose surfaces contain many small mirrors will be white. This is why foaming water is white, for it consists of innumerable little bubbles, and each bubble is a mirror, while before, the water as a whole was but one mirror.... [W]ater broken into distinct mirrors by bubbles therefore becomes white.... Such considerations make it clear that colors arise solely from a change of figure and position in a surface. If we had space, it would be easy to explain light, heat, and all qualities in the same way. Now if qualities are changed by motion alone, substance will also be changed by that very fact.... (L, 96–97)

8. PW, 176.
9. PW, 78

10. The nature of monadic expression is discussed in sections II and III of chapter six.
11. L, 339 (PW, 72).
12. LH, IV, vii, C 107v-108r (quoted in Mates, 225).
13. Mugnai, 49.
14. Grua, 535, as construed in Mates 60.
15. LLP, 135.
16. Woolhouse, 94. See also Gibson, 194.
17. Yet though I do not believe Locke reasons from (20) to (21), since some interpreters have asserted that he does, in section IX I sketch an alternative reconstruction of the IC argument in accord with that reading of Locke and with NPE read my way.
18. Locke, 319 (Book II, chap. 25, sec. 1).
19. Ibid.
20. Ibid., 320.
21. Ibid., 321.
22. In addition to (20), the second sentence also contains the claim that a change of *relation* can occur without a change in one of the things related. Further, as the first sentence expresses Locke's conception of extrinsic denominations *and* relations, it asserts more than just (21). It also contains the claim that relations are not in or are not properties of the things related. However, since, for purposes of interpreting Leibniz's NPE, the primary concern is Locke's view of extrinsic denominations, I am going to leave the claims about relations out of the discussion of Locke's argument for the moment. The corresponding claims about relations are discussed in a limited way in section VI of chapter four.
23. Someone might object to Locke's argument on the grounds that even if (21) is true and even if it is true that Caius's extrinsic denomination changes as a result of a change in his son, those facts do not by themselves guarantee that Caius has not changed. Suppose that, by sheer coincidence and not in any way a consequence of the death of his son, at the very moment Caius loses the extrinsic denomination <father>, one of the hairs on his head turns white. Then the change of extrinsic denomination has been accompanied by a change in Caius. I do not think, however, that such a possibility counts against the inference to (20). (20) only claims, and nothing Locke says implies anything stronger, that a change of extrinsic denomination *can* occur without a change occurring in the denominated thing. So, that changes of extrinsic denomination sometimes occur simultaneously with coincidental changes of intrinsic denomination does not defeat the argument. Of course, if things change constantly, if all things are in a constant state of flux, then that would defeat the argument. (20) would be false, even if (21) were true.
24. It is not clear why Locke confined himself to cases in which one of the things related ceases to exist. The same argument would seem to establish (20) in any instance of what I earlier labeled as type B cases, cases in which one's extrinsic denominations change as a result of a change in something else. For any change in one's extrinsic denominations that occurs as a result of a change in someone else, if the change of extrinsic denomination does not itself amount to a change in the denominated thing, then the extrinsic denomination can occur without a change in the de-

nominated thing. Leibniz appears to have realized this, for in the second instance of the IC argument quoted earlier, he speaks of a case in which his similitude to someone else arises solely by a change in the other person and without any change in himself. I take it the change in the other person need not have been his or her death. Thus, though I am not certain why Locke only speaks of (20) in connection with cases where one of the things related ceases to exist, it seems clear that he need not have.

25. NE, 227. The phrases in single quotes are direct quotes from Locke's section 1.
26. Ibid.
27. They could, of course, also deny that Locke accepted any inferential connection between (20) and (21). But I think this is implausible. It is highly probable that someone who accepted both claims, as Locke does, would regard them as inferentially connected in some way. And Locke's discussion in section 5 strongly supports the view that he regarded (21) as a reason for (20). In any event, denying an inferential connection between the two will not aid the reductionist in any way that I can see. The problems I raise against their view would, I believe, still apply, even if an inferential connection is denied.
28. See especially the statement of the argument given in LH, IV, vii, C 107v-108r (quoted in Mates, 225 and in section II above).
29. Locke, Book II, chap. 25, sec. 1. Jonathan Bennett has claimed that Locke held to a reductionist view of extrinsic denominations. Bennett, 254. Rae Langton has recently argued that, though Locke did not accept extrinsic denominations as properties, he also did not believe they were reducible to intrinsic denominations. Langton, 75–91. Even if Langton is right about Locke (and assuming, what is far less clear, that Leibniz read Locke the way that Langton does), though, it still makes little sense for Leibniz to assert reductionist NPE as a response to Locke in the context of type B changes.
30. Ibid.
31. Cover and O'Leary-Hawthorne, 76–77.
32. Mugnai would not accept this claim. Under Mugnai's view, since extrinsic denominations are included in individual concepts, propositions having them as predicate concepts can be true by virtue of PS. Thus, Mugnai, though he would surely accept (24) as expressing the import of NPE, would not necessarily be liable to this objection. His view of NPE, as discussed in section III of chapter four, still cannot ensure that extrinsic denominations have a foundation in what they denominate. Nor can his view otherwise provide a plausible reconstruction of the PS argument for NPE. For a showing of the latter, see the Appendix.
33. LH, IV, vii, C107v-108r (quoted in Mates, 225).

Chapter Five

1. L, 526–27.
2. PW, 133–34.
3. PW, 226 (L, 700), 227 (L, 701), among other places.
4. PW, 229 (L, 702). Nor is space a property of God (Ibid.).
5. L, 682 (PW, 221). See also, L, 700 (PW, 226): "space is nothing other than an order of the existence of things, which is observed when they exist simultaneously."

6. PW, 230 (L, 703). Mates also interprets the order of coexistence among objects to be their distances from one another (Mates, 229).
7. PW, 231 (L, 703).
8. Ibid., 231–32 (L, 703–4).
9. Ibid., 232 (L, 704). This passage is also quoted in chapter one (p. 7).
10. L, 609.
11. Mates, 210, n.4, and 234–35; Cover and Hawthorne, 72, n.22.
12. L, 500.
13. NE, 401.
14. PW, 60. Kulstad also employs this passage to show that, for Leibniz, any true predicate, including relational ones, are intrinsic denominations of the subjects of which they are true (Kulstad [1980], 427).
15. PW, 62 (L, 337).
16. As in the passage concerning the lengths of L and M (PW, 232).
17. L, 526–27.
18. As in the version of the IC argument found at LH, IV, vii, C107v-108r.
19. PW, 133.
20. I believe this statement of ID is sufficiently clear for present purposes. All the work that needs to be done on reconstructing the argument can be adequately accomplished with just this statement of it. Hence, I shall forego any further discussion of the principle.
21. PW, 133–34.
22. Strictly speaking, what follows is that their relations of situation will not agree, but this itself implies that they will have different relations of situation. The relations of situation of A and B can fail to agree only if there is a difference in their relations of situation.
23. There is a problem with Leibniz's reasoning in the ID argument. NPE is a general conclusion about extrinsic denominations, and even if Leibniz is successful in showing that NPE is true with respect to relations of situation, that will not show that NPE is true for other extrinsic denominations. I do not see any remedy for this defect, but I suspect that Leibniz would have thought that if NPE were true for some extrinsic denominations, then there would be no reason that it should not be true for all. In any case, this defect will exist regardless of which version of NPE is adopted.
24. Cover and Hawthorne, 72, n.22. They also claim that when Leibniz says extrinsic denominations are included in complete individual concepts, he means that the intrinsic denominations that provide the foundation for extrinsic denominations are included in those concepts (69–70).
25. Ibid., 72, n.22.
26. Ibid., 66. Mates also seems to claim this (214–15).

Chapter Six

1. L, 207.
2. L, 339.
3. PW, 176.
4. McRae, 23, 42.

5. Swoyer (1995b), 81, 86–87.
6. In addition to Swoyer (ibid.), see Mates, 38; Sleigh (1990), 174; and Kulstad (1977), 74–75, though Kulstad, on p. 76, n.39, appears willing to entertain the possibility that the isomorphism view might be correct.
7. Mates, 38.
8. Swoyer (1995b), 79–84.
9. The best general discussions of Leibnizian expression are found in Swoyer (ibid.), and Kulstad (1977).
10. Leibniz sometimes states that it is monads or souls themselves that express the other monads (L, 339 [PW, 72], 649 [PW, 189]; PW, 176). At other times he says that it is the complete individual concepts of these monads that express the universe (L, 269 [PW, 90], 524). I believe he intends to assert that both are the case. If he did not mean to assert both, then he was speaking loosely in one of the two lines of texts. Yet I can find no principled grounds in Leibniz's writings for deciding which of the two it is. Indeed, there are even passages where he comes extremely close to asserting both in the same paragraph:

> Each substance has something of the infinite in so far as it involves its cause, God; i.e. it has some trace of omniscience and omnipotence. For in the perfect notion of each individual substance there are contained all its predicates, both necessary and contingent, past, present and future; indeed, each substance expresses the whole universe according to its position and point of view, in so far as the others are related to it. (PW, 77)

See also section 8 of the *Discourse* (L, 307–8 [PW, 17–18])
11. PW, 176; L, 649.
12. PW, 187 (L, 648). See also PW, 77, 176.
13. Of course, in order for a monad A to express *every* other monad in this way, it must be the case that for every other monad B there is at least one extrinsic denomination that relates A to B and which is true of A (i.e., included in A's concept). As will soon be discussed, Leibniz explicitly furnishes this claim as a premise in his argument from NPE to expression.
14. L, 524.
15. See chapter three, pp. 39–42 for a discussion of concept inclusion.
16. Mates, 220
17. On the notion of one concept's being a component of another, see note 19 of chapter three.
18. DSR, 83–85.
19. PW, 90 (L, 269). At the end of the selection, Leibniz says that he establishes monadic expression in other ways. Indeed, the NPE argument is neither his only nor his most commonly given argument for expression. Most often, he invokes the interconnection of all things to prove expression. For instances of this argument, see PW, 176 and L, 648–49 (PW, 187–89).
20. Put this way, (26) bears a superficial similarity to Leibniz's doctrine of the connection of all things. Sleigh, in fact, equates (26) with this doctrine (Sleigh [1990], 175). I believe this is a mistake. Leibniz's most explicit discussions of the doctrine of

the connection of all things, as shown in section II of chapter four, reveal that it is the claim that a change in one monad entails a change in every other. (26) is simply not that claim. Nor is (26) logically equivalent to that claim. For it would seem that a monad could change *without* a change occurring in every other, even if (26) was true. That is, if B were to change in some way having nothing to do with the manner in which D relates it to A, why should we suppose that A would also change? In any case, I believe, (26) adequately reflects the meaning of the premise Leibniz actually gives in *Primary Truths,* and that is what is most important here.

21. For a discussion of the conceptual structure of extrinsic denominations and Leibniz's probable view on the matter, see section IV of chapter three.

22. A function that accomplishes this could perhaps be defined as follows: Let R be a binary relation and let D<x> be the extrinsic denomination of bearing R to an individual x. Then the relevant function F from a thing's extrinsic denominations to the concepts of other individuals that are components of those denominations is F(D<x>) = <x>. Thus, F(<lover of Helen>) = <Helen>.

23. Sleigh (1990), 77.
24. Ibid., 176.
25. L, 339 (PW, 72); L, 457 (PW, 122); PW, 77, among others.
26. Sleigh (1990), 77, 175–76.
27. Cf. Sleigh's rendering (Ibid., 76).
28. Ibid., 77.
29. Ibid., 77–78.
30. I know of only one interpreter, Parkinson, who attributes the strong view to Leibniz, and even he only seems to do so on the basis that Leibniz's acceptance of the weak view and his acceptance of the doctrine of monadic expression *commit* him to the strong view. See Parkinson, 149–50.
31. PW, 19 (L, 308). Emphasis added. See also PW, 176 and L, 649 (PW, 188–89), among others.
32. PW, 201 (L, 640). See also PW, 77.
33. Incidentally, Sleigh does not refer to weak expression as such because it claims that monads express some truths about the others rather than all. Sleigh refers to it as weak because in contrast to strong expression, weak expression allows monads to express the universe without even low-level cognition of what they express (Sleigh [1990], 176).
34. Ibid., 77.
35. Ibid. In this, Sleigh shows an awareness of the point made in section III of chapter six that monads express other monads through their extrinsic denominations.
36. Ibid., 175.
37. Ibid.
38. PW, 197. Quoted by Sleigh (1990), 175.
39. PW, 122 (L, 457).
40. Sleigh (1990), 175.
41. Ibid.
42. See note 30 of chapter six.
43. Mates, 80–83, 220. Cover and Hawthorne appear to take the same view. Cover and Hawthorne, 73–77.
44. Mates, 80–83, 220.

Appendix

1. Mugnai, 117.
2. Ibid., 121–22.
3. Ibid., 49
4. NE, 227.
5. PW, 89 (L, 268).
6. Loemker's translation makes Leibniz's separation of the two claims even more evident: "It follows further that there are no purely extrinsic denominations which have no basis at all in the denominated thing itself. For the concept of the denominated subject necessarily involves the concept of the predicate. Likewise, whenever the denomination of a thing is changed, some variation has to occur in the thing itself" (L, 268).
7. See Mates, 5. For evidence of Leibniz's general commitment to the close ties between metaphysics and logic, see G, IV, 292.
8. Mugnai, 129.
9. Ibid.
10. PW, 133.
11. This is how the respective showings of my version of NPE and reductionist NPE are handled in chapter five.

Index

a priori proof, 23–25, 116n26
accidents, 6; distinguished from properties, 114n37; relational, 7. *See also* individual accidents, doctrine of
Adams, Robert, 116n30, 119n25
analyses, of concepts, 24, 28–29, 39–40; infinite in the case of contingent propositions, 116n26; of relational propositions into non-relational ones, 5–6
Aristotle, 24

Bennett, Jonathan, 122n29
Broad, C. D., 22, 115n20
Brown, Gregory, 118n5
Burdick, Howard, 112n21

change, as motion, 49, 120n7
complete individual concepts, definition of, 11–12, 19, 111n6; not included in extrinsic denominations, 8, 35, 39–42, 88
concepts, inclusion relation among, 8, 13, 35, 39–41, 119n19; L's logic of, 39–45; simple and complex, 28–29, 39. *See also* complete individual concepts; oblique addition; real addition
contingent truths. *See* truths
Cover, Jan and John Hawthorne, 2, 5, 8, 19–22, 25, 29, 35–38, 41–42, 65, 74, 80–81, 99, 112n24, 112n27, 114n7, 115n13, 115n15, 115n16, 118n1, 119n20, 122n 31, 123n11, 123n24, 125n43
D'Agostino, Fred, 9, 113n29
denominations, definition of, 3. *See also* extrinsic denominations; intrinsic denominations

expression, general, 84–85; monadic, 2, 12, 33–34, 50, 77–78, 83, 85–97, 104–105; and
perception, 91, 94; strong, 91, 94–97; weak, 91–94
extrinsic denominations, construed as extrinsic to what they denominate, 12, 75–76; construed as relational properties, 1, 3; as the foundations of relations simpliciter, 74–79. *See also* denominations; intrinsic denominations

foundations, of relations, 9–11, 64, 69–81; of truth, 21–29, 31–32

Gibson, James, 121n16

Hintikka, Jaakko, 113n35
Hippocrates, 49

identity of indiscernibles, principle of, 2, 69, 77, 104, 123n20
individual accidents, doctrine of, 2, 6, 34
interconnection of all things, doctrine of, 2, 49–50, 117n42
intrinsic denominations, construed as non-relational properties, 1, 3; construed as intrinsic to what they denominate, 75–76, 123n14 ; as the foundations of extrinsic
denominations, 9–11, 21–22, 66, 70–81. *See also* denominations; extrinsic denominations

Ishiguro, Hide, 111n3, 112n27, 113n34

Kulstad, Mark, 6–7, 111n2, 112n8, 112n22, 113n35, 115n12, 123n14, 124n6, 124n9

Langton, Rae, 122n29
Locke, John, 48, 53–55, 58, 64–65, 122n29

Mates, Benson, 3–4, 74, 85, 87–88, 96, 99, 111n1, 111n2, 111n7, 112n12, 112n15, 112n24, 114n7, 116n30, 118n5, 119n12, 121n12, 121n14, 123n6, 123n11, 123n26, 124n6
McCullough, Lawrence, 112n21
McRae, Robert, 123n4
monads, each a world apart, 9
Mugnai, Massimo, 2, 52, 99–105, 114n37, 121n13, 122n32, 126n1, 126n2, 126n3, 126n8, 126n9

necessary truths. *See* truths

oblique addition, 45. *See also* concepts, L's logic of

Parkinson, G. H. R., 95, 112n15, 125n30
plenum, 49–50, 120n5
predicate-in-subject principle, definition of, 13; applicability to propositions containing extrinsic denominations, 14–32
predicates, L's allowance of relational ones, 5, 14, 18–20, 115n8
propositions, identical, 24–29, 52; subject-predicate view of, 5, 7, 16, 115n8

real addition, 39–45. *See also* concepts, L's logic of
reductionist interpretation of NPE, description of, 1, 3–4; textual case for, 4–11; weak vs. strong, 91–92, 95–96
relations, ideality of, 6, 58–59; simpliciter distinguished from relational accidents, 7, 35. *See also* foundations, of relations
Rescher, Nicholas, 114n6, 114n7, 119n11
Russell, Bertrand, 4, 42, 99, 111n7, 112n9, 114n6, 114n8
Russell-Couturat thesis, 42, 99

Sleigh, Robert, 84, 90–97, 115n20, 124n6, 124n20, 125n23, 125n24, 125n26, 125n27, 125n28, 125n29, 125n33, 125n34, 125n35, 125n36, 125n37, 125n38, 125n40, 125n41
space, L's view of, 71–74, 76–81
substance, Aristotelian view of, 8, 38
sufficient reason, principle of. *See* truth, reason for
Swoyer, Chris, 40, 84–85, 119n8, 119n11, 119n14, 119n16, 119n17, 124n5, 124n6, 124n8, 124n9

time, 71, 76–77, 104
truth, reason for, 21–32, 52. *See also* foundations, of truth; predicate-in-subject principle
truths, contingent, 15, 22, 116n26, 116n35; necessary, 15, 22, 116n26

Woolhouse, R. S., 54, 121n16